Talking with Bob & Doris

RECOLLECTIONS OF EAST SUFFOLK LIFE

Bob & Doris Ling
in conversation with
Eric Crozier

Edited and introduced
by Simon Loftus

Peninsular

First published in Great Britain in 1987
Revised edition published in 2022 by Peninsular Books
Bulcamp House, Halesworth, Suffolk IP19 9LG

Copyright © Peninsular Books 1987/2022

ISBN 978-1-871003-01-7

Designed by Spring, Southwold

Printed and bound by
Short Run Press Ltd, Exeter

In memoriam

Bob Ling
1923 – 2010

Doris Ling
1920 – 2011

A note on the revised edition

The recordings on which these transcripts were based were made by Eric Crozier during the winter of 1985/86 and edited for publication by Simon Loftus.

This revised and enlarged edition contains only minor changes to the original text but includes additional matter, notably extracts from letters to Benjamin Britten and Imogen Holst written by Doris Ling and conserved in the Britten-Pears Archive. Thanks to Judith Ratcliffe, Archivist. I have also written a new Introduction.

High resolution digital images of old family photos were kindly supplied by Tony Ling, to whom many thanks.

S. L.

Contents

Past midnight, at the end of another hard-working day at Snape Maltings

Introduction by Simon Loftus

Remembering Bob & Doris

Here is a fragment from the conversations that Bob and Doris Ling recorded with Eric Crozier, long ago. Bob is talking: "When Ben [Britten] had a performance at the hall, he used to pop in to see us on the way from his dressing room, and he'd say: 'Get me a whisky, will you Bob, so I can have a wet when I come off stage?' Other times he would say: 'Come and listen to the bittern', and we would go outside and hear the old bittern booming." Which prompts Doris to recall the time that the Queen Mother came to Snape and "we were cleaning late one night, and the bittern was booming away like a foghorn."

I can hear the weaving together of their two voices, the sound of an almost vanished Suffolk, an earthiness, a relish for life – the 'wet' after work, the boom of the 'old bittern' across the marshes. And I am reminded how much their life was rooted in this particular place, which they loved so much.

They were born locally, in great rural poverty, and Bob started work at the Maltings as a fifteen-year-old boy, in 1938 – as his father, grandfather and great-grandfather had done. He could remember the time when "there were four drying rooms where the concert hall is now, with eight large furnaces underneath", for Snape supplied malt to brewers as far distant as London, sending it down river on the wherries. The place was its own social world, with sports clubs and concert parties and pantomimes, to provide light relief from the fierce physical labour. And it was at Snape village hall that Bob first met Doris, when he left his "little girl friend" (Doris's words) and made a beeline for this self-possessed eighteen-year-old with a bunch of violets pinned to her hip and her hair done in a Marcel wave. "I suppose Bob thought that was the height of sophistication." He lied about his age (he was three years younger than her) and soon they were courting. That was the beginning of one of the world's great love stories.

It survived the war, when Bob served in converted trawlers, sweeping for mines out towards Iceland (while Doris was left to look after their first son) and it survived the devastation when the Maltings suddenly shut down, in 1965. It survived the years when they worked together as gravediggers, and the day that Bob's spade struck a wasps' nest and he almost died from the stings, and the night when they looked out from their little bungalow on Snape Terrace to see the recently converted concert hall consumed by fire. And it survived what they both thought was the worst time of their lives, when they did a milk round, and grew to hate the smell of stale milk, the biting dogs, the bad payers, the repetitive monotony. Finally they struck lucky, for in 1971 Bob and Doris were taken on at the Concert Hall, to help out backstage, and three months later they were put in charge. They stayed for nearly twenty years, becoming an inseparable part of the legends of Aldeburgh and Snape.

Partly it was to do with their extraordinary capacity for friendship – with everyone from the most timid student to the sometimes difficult Britten – and partly their devotion to the place where they did everything from shifting scenery to cleaning the loos, to welcoming the Queen Mother. But what was even more special, for all their friends, was their 'largeness of heart' – as was said of another famous figure in Snape's history, the great Newson Garrett. The sound of Bob and Doris telling their stories together, voices leaping and laughing as they recalled the ups and downs of their life, pungent and wickedly funny, or Doris's wonderful letters, talking as if you were next to her, distilled an astonishing generosity.

I was recently re-reading one of those letters, written at four in the morning – after an evening spent together with me and Irène, and Hugh and Tricia Maguire, in August 1989. Bob must have been asleep (having serenaded Doris on the harmonica, as he did every night when they went to bed) but she was still turning over in her mind all the things that she had enjoyed that day, and she wrote this lovely dreamy sentence. "I know life can be so very hard and cruel but it is a strange and wondrous thing too isn't it."

When Bob died at the age of 87, just before Christmas 2010, Doris found that her zest for life was gone. Heartbroken, she followed him three weeks later. They are buried together at Snape.

The boy Bob, c. 1930

1

"We were very poor"

BOB: I began at Blaxhall 'High' School; they called it that because it's up a little hill. I started there before I was five. There was quite a crowd of us kids living down there at Stone Common and we had a mile to walk to school. We were very poor – really poor. On Thursdays the grocer from Woodbridge, Tyson's, came round in his van and we had a quarter of sweets to share out amongst three of us (my sister Iris wasn't born then), about five sweets each to last a week. We didn't get pocket money, and we never had bread, butter and jam – either bread and marge, or bread and jam. We took our sandwiches to school wrapped up in newspaper, and it was bitterly cold sitting in the classroom at lunchtime in our little boots, eating them. There was another family of Lings living near the church in Blaxhall on a part called the Knoll, thirteen of them, and their father worked for Lord Ullswater, and he used to go and see the cook and get lovely pork dripping, and we always envied them because they had what we called 'Lord Ullswater's dripping' to spread on their bread, lovely and thick and white.

Mrs Newby, the head teacher at Blaxhall, was a tremendous woman and she sometimes gave us a special treat: she would come through the door with a basket of apples and throw them into the playground and we would all scramble for them. I only went to Blaxhall School for two years, but I vividly remember sitting in the hedge with terrible headaches. When I went to school at Snape – I was seven – they found I needed glasses, so fitted me out with a pair which I left about all over the place because I hated wearing them. We used to go and sweep leaves up for Dad to rot down on his garden and allotment – this was in the evenings, and very often along Crisp's Lane (or Mark Newsom's Lane as it was called then) between Snape and the Aldeburgh road, we would sweep up the Aldeburgh road, we would sweep up the leaves and collect them in sacks and I would take my glasses off and put them in the hedge -then I'd remember in the middle of the night and have to get up very early and go and look for them before going to school – and I always found them.

Stanley Reeve was our master at Snape – very strict he was: and there was a *gross* of children, 144 of them, I have always remembered, in three classes. He used the stick very severely, but he was a brilliant teacher. Once a week he and the woodwork teacher took us up to the old school-building opposite Snape Church Garage, and we made all the equipment, a vaulting horse and all that stuff, for our PT. We made two sectional huts: they were brought down to the school – and we had account books to teach us book-keeping through rearing fowls and selling the eggs. We even did a biology lesson once and cut a chicken in half.

Stanley Reeve was a great swimmer. He taught us to swim in the river down here, and we made our own springboard at the woodwork class and a raft and two changing huts with duckboards and everything. There was a big gala each year and we had a race – two hundred yards – between Snape bridge and the railway bridge. We had a greasy pole, too! I remember coming third in the race for boys under fourteen and winning sixpence, but they ran out of prize money, so I had to wait until nearly dark to get my sixpence.

DORIS: I often wonder about education. Was Bob a determined type of boy from the time he was born? Was that *in* him . . . ? Or was it the influence of Mr Reeve made him into this can't-sit-down-got-to-be-at-work kind of man?

BOB: Mr Reeve caned me more than any other boy in the school, but I respected him all the same. He used to take me to Norwich Football in the dickey of his old Singer car – there were no car heaters then – me and another lad sitting in the back with our scarves around our necks. That was wonderful for boys like us, for Norwich was then in the First Division.

ERIC: Did you resent being poor, or take it for granted?

BOB: No, I have never resented it. I think it made me fight for survival, though. Maybe that is why I find money hard to spend. My wants are so small. If nobody bought me a Christmas present, it wouldn't worry me a bit. My son rang the other day to ask, "What can we buy you for Christmas?", and I had to tell him I didn't really want anything.

DORIS: If only we could go back to the old days of a walk on the beach, a piece of beef, and church, I think the world would be a better place . . .

BOB: I used to love preparing for Christmas. We got so excited looking for bits of holly or for mistletoe in an old apple tree – it would take days! And carol-singing! The carol-singers in Snape were very well organised: they would go round visiting all the big houses, and old Harry Wright who sold firewood used to lend his horse and cart and take us over to Blackheath Mansion where Captain Vernon Wentworth played the organ and we sang our carols, then he brought round hot punch and mince pies. We thought that was marvellous! It was a long flat cart and we all sat on it, men and women too, and away we went down that immensely long drive from the Aldeburgh road to the bank of the river where Blackheath Mansion stands.

I was in the church choir, too, up at Snape. They paid us one penny a service as long as we attended choir practice. But one day we got a shilling, when Miss Thompson who played the organ (she had a twin sister) got married, and one thing we had to learn for that was *Lead on the breath, O God.* I enjoyed singing in the choir.

DORIS: Bob had a lovely voice. An such enthusiasm!

BOB: I didn't like school – well, not arithmetic and things like that. When that came along, I used to put my hand up and ask: "Please, sir, can I clean the drains?" Spelling, too, I didn't like – but I did the book-keeping for the chickens and Mr Reeve taught us to do sums. There were fifty in our class, so he would go all round – "Fifteen! . . . Seven!" – and we had to add the figures up. But he was always very strict. One April Fool's Day when I was about thirteen, nearly leaving school, he came out of his house and I asked him: "What kind of bird is that, sir?", and he answered, "I don't see any bird". So I said "April Fool!" He grabbed me by the scruff of the neck and frogmarched me into school and gave me the biggest caning I ever had, on my hands, with a big knobbed stick. I had to sit on my hands all afternoon. They were terrible!

ERIC: Were you beaten at home, too?

BOB: My father was very strict, but not too bad really. He would give us a thrashing if we came home late with wet feet: we used to go down to the marshes jumping ditches and invariably we would land in the middle, and then we sat and wrung out our socks and put them to dry because we were scared to go home – and Dad would be sitting there waiting for us and give us a ding round the ear, but nothing drastic . . . I reminded Stanley Reeve many years later, when I came out of the Navy, of how I caught him out on April Fool's Day, but he couldn't remember it at all. So I told him, "You know why, sir? Because *you* were at the other end of the stick!"

ERIC: But you admired him?

BOB: I did. He is still alive, over 80 now, must be 85, and he hasn't long retired. When he gave up as headmaster at Kesgrave Modern School, he worked for an accountant in Ipswich.

DORIS: The lessons I hated most was Sir Walford Davies doing music on the radio, because I had no sense of pitch. In fact, I was turned out of the church choir when we were first married. Bob was in the choir, so "You come along" he said. Mr Mann, the choirmaster, bless his heart, was ever so tactful: he suggested some of us should go down into the body of the church to help the congregation, but I was the only one who was picked! It was a polite way of turning me out, because I really can't sing for toffee.

ERIC: Did you ever have holidays?

BOB: Yes! We used to go away once a year to my grandma's at Norton, near Bury St Edmunds, and that was a big treat. Nana Bradbrook was her name. Her first husband, Bloomfield, was killed in a chalk pit, buried alive, and she married again. Emma her name was, and that's the name of our youngest granddaughter.

My uncle, who was single, worked for the Tomlin family at the hall at Ixworth, and he used to give us a ha'penny every now and then, and a great aunt of ours owned a little sweet shop across the road from my grandma's, and we used to buy sherbet fountains there. You bit the end off the liquorice and sucked up the sherbet until you nearly choked!

DORIS: Bob's family were divided absolutely in half. On his mother's side they were very reserved, very quiet: on the other side they were pub-going people, out for a laugh and a dance.

BOB: My father was a big British Legion man, out nearly every night.

DORIS: They all were in those days!

BOB: They used to have their step-dances and that down at the Ship Inn at Blaxhall. *(The Sheep Inn was locally pronounced 'Ship".)*

DORIS: We never had a week's holiday. My father used to hire a big bus, a coach, and take all the family to Yarmouth for the day. That was our outing: we all used to go, sisters, brothers, aunts. There was a fish restaurant in Yarmouth

Bob's parents on their wedding day, 1919, with (standing left to right)
Grandmother and Grandad Ling, Bob's uncle Willie Bloomfield, Grandad and
Nana Bradbrook, "On his mother's side they were very reserved, very quiet: on
the other side they were pub-going people, out for a laugh and a dance."

High Street, so Dad booked a whole room and paid for it out of his tips from people playing tennis. That was the highlight of our year. There would be forty or fifty of us with the children, and all the people living round would come to wave us off.

BOB: I loved going to Norton, because my grandmother lived in a big house with a marvellous thatch. It was called *The Wash*, and at the back was a big wash-room like a long passage with a white brick floor and a bowl and a tap, all smelling of soap, and that was where you scrubbed yourself up. It was a lovely place to keep stuff, too – the ham or beef was kept there, and the bicycles . . . we used to go there for a month, so mother could see *her* mother and all the family, and Dad stayed at home and looked after himself. We went by train. We got to Campsea Ashe station in an old Morris Cowley, with a big bull-nosed brass front. Mrs Gaze was the only person in Blaxhall who owned a car, and she took the whole family for sixpence. At the other end, a Mr Salmon, who owned a nursery near my grandmother, came to pick us up at Elmswell station in *his* old Morris Cowley.

There was a big old pear-tree in the garden there and a stream they got the water from, and I loved diving in and going for a swim – they had quite a job to keep me out of it. We used to go in the harvest-fields, too, chasing rabbits.

2

"I ought to have been a boy"

DORIS: We never had a holiday like that – just the one day each year . . . My mother went out to work as an undercook at ten years old, and on her days off they would go back to Thorpeness and grandma would set them to pick stones from the fields.

I had a marvellous mother, but if we weren't well, with being women and the time of the month, and I said, "Oh Mum, I don't feel well today", she would ask, "Are you ill enough for the doctor? – "No, but I feel rotten." – "If you are not ill enough for the doctor you get to work – or get to school" – or something else! She always had to work, and we were brought up to do the same. She had a hard life, because my grandfather was a fisherman up at Thorpeness and that wasn't easy.

All our family went to Aldeburgh School from the age of three – three to fourteen. There was Miss Marsh, Miss Cooper and Mr Witham, and they were marvellous. I was very fond of school; it was never a hardship to me. My youngest brother – I don't say he was spoiled, but he didn't like school and he didn't want to go, so I have to spend a long time sitting in the Infants' Class with him or he would have run away – he had to have someone of the family there. He is two years younger than me, so I must have been five or six then.

ERIC: Is that where you learned to like reading?

DORIS: Well, being a big family we all tended to be readers. When I was young I used to read *Red Letter* and *Woman's Weekly*, which gave me a wrong attitude to life and marriage altogether. I thought it was all going to be Romance. I remember walking up the aisle thinking, I'm getting married now and I am going to be made a fuss of for the rest of my life!

My childhood was wonderful. The older ones had a harder time, but by the time I came along (I was the seventh) they were out at work and bringing money home. When I went into service I got five shillings a week. Mum gave me two shillings back – a shilling for the pictures and a shilling for my clothing club – and she kept the rest although I wasn't living at home any longer. That was what everyone did; when their turn came to earn money, they all had to help. I really loved school and didn't want to leave at all. English was always my best subject. We had to write a composition once on *The View from My Window* – and there was a field of mustard and beyond that the sun coming up across the river: so I wrote about that and mine was best – probably because I'd read all those romantic books. I love words. Sometimes when Peter *(Pears)* used to read to us, I could have listened all day. History, too – I loved that as well.

We were a large family, and I was lucky because several of my brothers and sisters were out at work already, so I benefited by getting more presents at Christmas, Easter and birthdays than my schoolmates with smaller families. But then I had to go into domestic service myself, and when I came home the first Christmas the presents stopped because I was working: so all I got was a box of handkerchiefs from mother and a pair of lisle stockings from my granny, and to me that was the worst Christmas of my life: it was as if an exciting bubble had suddenly burst.

There were thirteen of us children – eight girls and five boys, so with granny that made sixteen. The boys slept in the attic, we girls in one bed, and granny at the foot of our bed in a single bed, and the smaller children were in mum and dad's room. Dad was secretary to lots of organisations in Aldeburgh, and he used to go out most nights: all the men did in those days, but mother and granny were always there. Mum was ever so strict, but a lovely woman with it – well, she had to be strict with so many of us. Our house was on the way down to Slaughden, where the old mill is, near the Latymer Club, and that is where they had the fair. We used to lie in bed when we were children and watch the people going up and down on the horses, reflected on the ceiling.

We were a lovely happy family, and even now if we go to weddings – or funerals, for that matter – we always get together and talk about those days – how strict mum was, and dad . . . We had to clean the shoes on a Sunday, take it in turns, and if you hadn't done that bit at the bottom you had to go back and do them again. Dad had been in the Fourth Cycles, the Territorials, then he went to the Yorks and Lancs Regiment, and then he had his leg blown off on the Somme. He brought thirteen of us up, and he only had one leg, and he used to work at the tennis-courts, and I have seen him come home midday, take his sock off – blood from the rawness of the wound in the heat – have it dressed and go back to work. He never gave in. He was ever such a man, a typical sergeant-major.

BOB: He was the type of man . . . well, when I came on leave during the war, I would go down to the United Services Club, and there would be five or six of us with him and we would treat each other so in the finish we had had six or seven pints – too much, really – and we used to walk from the Slaughden end up to the Leiston Road . . .

DORIS: We had moved by then . . .

BOB: We would all be falling about a bit, but Woffy, when he got near the door, would pull himself up and be as right as rain, while we were all falling about and talking nonsense. Doris's mum used to think *we* had been drinking and he hadn't!

ERIC: What name did you call him?

DORIS: Woffy. My brother Bill who used to work here was called Woffy, too. Mr Hubbard, who had the electrical shop in Saxmundham, he has a racehorse and he named it Woffy, and last week he took my brother and his wife up to Worlingworth to see it. The horse is going to be raced this Saturday.

ERIC: Why 'Woffy', though?

DORIS: Because of his initials. He was William Oliver Fryer: so they called him 'Woffy' at school. My mum was Alice Jemima, and my grandma was Eliza, and I always wanted my grandchildren to be called the same, but they are Charlotte and Emma, Stephen and Sean. I started going out to work when I was fourteen. I wanted to work in a shop, that was always my dream, but in those days you didn't have any choice. I was going to work for one lady, a woman on her own, and mother said we'd go and see her on the Tuesday, but she didn't take me with her – I don't know why. She went on her own, and she saw a mouse run across the kitchen table: so that was the end of that. Then there was a family with five – no, six – children and a seventh on the way: so mum said – you go there, that will help that woman, and I went and lived in. We had to work hard with such a big family, and I used to knit at night for the new baby that was coming.

My sisters went into service – two of them worked for Lady Eddis – where there were footmen and butlers and things: they were all right because they had these young lads and girls to laugh with – but I was in the era when you got five shillings weekly and you were in blue uniform in the morning and black at night – and you were on your own. I went from the freedom of being able to do my own thing (strict though mum was about the time I came back at night) into service, and I never was fond of housework anyway, and I could only go out on Tuesday afternoons – and that did something to me I have never forgotten . . . This was 1934. It was a lonely time for me, because if I had gone into the bigger kind of service like my sisters, I would have had company. I remember how I had to wash the tea-towels and rinse them five times until the water was clear, and if the lady of the house tested them and the water was cloudy, my! I'd get into trouble! She was very thorough and that was good training – but it was lost on me because I wasn't the type to knuckle under. I rebelled against it – and if I had an afternoon off and went home, I had to clean Mum's kitchen and wash up, anyway, because she had gone to chapel. Mum worked terribly hard, but they used to go to chapel . . . We used to baby-sit for our sisters, too.

When I was much younger, I was always farmed out. I had an aunt with a daughter who went to hospital – so I went to live with the aunt. Then I went to Martlesham to a relative whose husband was away digging water-wells, and there were tramps about – so I lived with her for a while. Then I went to Knodishall, because the woman there went into hospital and her daughter had got stepbrothers. Then I went to Leiston because my Aunt Annie was in hospital, and for breakfast each morning I went up the garden to pick two bantam's eggs out of the nest. This was all before I left school, of course.

The lady I worked for was strict but ever so nice. It wasn't her fault: it was my nature. I've always valued freedom above everything, and I didn't have it. Really I ought have been a boy and gone into the Forces.

3

"We got married"

DORIS: I first met Bob at Snape. The village hall here had a terrible reputation for wildness. They used to have local dances, a shilling each dance, and the Blaxhall boys came and they used to fight. One time I was there, they had such a fight one of them spun right across the billiard table and tore the green baize. My mother wouldn't let us go there, but at the time my brother Fred was home on leave from the Grenadier Guards and he said: "I'll take them, mum. Me and Jess Smith are going, I'll look after them." So they brought us in the car, me and my friend, dumped us at the village hall, then they went down to the Crown Inn and that was the last we saw of them.

In those days I had a black dress with a bunch of real Parma violets (threepence from Hallas's in Aldeburgh) pinned on the hip, and I used to have my hair done with a Marcel wave, and I suppose to Bob that was the height of sophistication. He was only fifteen, but he had a little girl-friend here. He was always old for his age – I though he was eighteen and I never did know for ages he was only fifteen – and he left his little girl-friend I didn't know about and asked me to dance. He was very smart in those days and always held himself well, though his clothes weren't the best, and he said, can I see you again? So I said: "Well, not over here, but I'm down Aldeburgh a lot", and the next night he and another boy came down. He used to come every night except Monday and then he would write me a letter and send it by a girl who worked at the laundry. But when I began to get used to him and I was afraid he would get used to me, I used to hide behind the lifeboat for about ten minutes, so he would think I was late and begin to get worried. I think I was the boss in those days – which seems incredible looking back.

When we thought we would get engaged we asked Bob's mum and she said "Don't talk nonsense!" There was a lovely ring in Stephenson's and I said

Bob and Doris on their wedding day, 12 April 1941

to Bob: "We'll get engaged without anyone knowing." My mum, of course, still thought Bob was eighteen. So I bought this ring and Bob paid me back a shilling a week, and we went to one of the shelters on the beach and got engaged all very nice. Then my mum said: "We'll have a party", and we had one at my house – they never did have them then in halls – and mum said: "I don't know what Bob's mum and dad are like. It's strange they don't even come to his engagement party" – but it was obvious they didn't know about it, anyway. They did eventually find out, because I had my photograph taken in a black costume with my ring prominently displayed against the skirt, and I suppose by then his mum knew me better and accepted me. When we got married finally, we were in the vestry and my brother-in-law who was best man said: "Look, Bob's put his age wrong!" – so I hissed "Shut up!" and put my hand over the register and my parents never did know he was only just eighteen. He had to take a note to the vicar with his dad's permission. The war was on and we wanted to belong together.

Bob was born 1923 and I was three years older. To be truthful, I had just been jilted when I first met him and I wanted to show this other chap I didn't care. Then I got very jealous when he was going into the navy – I was scared that might be the last I would see of him. Before he enlisted, Bob had a dream one night: he told me "I dreamed we went to live in Deeker Blower's farm over there", so when we were going round the village looking for somewhere to live we went to Deeker Blowers, but he said "Oh, no, I can't let you have that cottage of mine. I keep my corn in that" – but seeing how disappointed Bob was, he said "Well, if you'll help me to shift the corn, you can have it."

We got married in April 1941. I remember Bob and I walked to Aldeburgh one day when the snow was too bad for cycling and we had to shelter under a holly bush from some big German bombers flying over. When he came home on leave, Bob used to ride with no lights on his bike and the sentries would challenge him in the darkness.

4

"Making our own pleasures"

DORIS: I was thinking about what different lives youngsters have nowadays. When I was at school I had to take turns going with my father to the tennis courts. They had those red courts. This shows what my character is, because I had a string round my waist with a pole and two hessian sacks opened up and sewn together, and I had to go up and down the courts sweeping the footprints out, and I used to be thinking "Why should *I* have to do this, when those youngsters of exactly my age are sitting on the veranda having ginger beer and biscuits. *They* made the mess: why aren't they clearing it up?" Bob used to go round selling sweet-peas, but he didn't mind – that shows the difference in our characters.

BOB: Father used to grow salmon-coloured sweet peas, and times were tremendously hard: so he used to send me out with a box on a string round my neck to sell little bunches of mixed sweet peas, and the salmon ones cost a penny more. I would go round selling them on Saturday mornings.

DORIS: Bob has got a lovely attitude to life. I envy him, because he doesn't worry. Right from the time he was born he has revelled in hard work. I have always been his apprentice, and I've enjoyed it – everybody is good to me.

BOB: I remember one autumn we were courting in blackberry time. We weren't working Sundays then, and it was a good opportunity to get some blackberries, so we went out and picked sixty or seventy pounds to sell for dye. When I was a kid there used to be a man come to Blaxhall Stone Common in an old lorry with big green barrels and they used to tip the berries in those to make dye.

DORIS: One Sunday when our boys were young we went off for a picnic on our bikes and thoroughly enjoyed ourselves, and we picked these two big pails and Bob took them to sell and he got such a good price he came back and said we might as well finish the lot – and that spoiled our picnic because it was *pick, pick, pick* and the novelty had worn off.

BOB: Wally Smith 'Bunks' used to have a shop halfway up Snape Hill, opposite Ben Britten's mill, and Vic Last started his fried fish shop up there in a little wooden hut, and on the same side as Ben's mill there used to be a little pork butcher's shop. At that time there were two fish shops in Snape. Down in Snape Street the cottages came right across the road, so there was only room for one car to go through. You can still see where the cottages were cut off, just by the Parish noticeboard – they used to nearly meet in the middle. We played with our tops in the road in those days, and we could play for two hours up by the village hall without being disturbed, and if a van did come along you could hear it for miles. Martin's of Saxmundham had one of the first vans. Wells, the ironmongers, used to come round with paraffin and we would get a ride back to Saxmundham for the 'pictures', which were shown in the market hall. The first film I ever saw was *Tom Mix*. We would ride in with Wells for threepence and walk home. There was a big old draper's shop in Snape opposite the Crown – that was pulled down. When I went to school in Snape, there were six hundred inhabitants, and the school had 144 children in three classes. Now it has 35.

DORIS: We were sixteen in our family, as I told you, but it was nothing out of the way for a sister-in-law and a brother and two children to come for the weekend. There was always food, always room: we used to sleep five in a bed with our feet sticking out. We didn't wait to be invited. I might say to Bob: "I'm fed up!": so he would say: "Let us go and have a week-end at Aldeburgh." I just don't know how my mother coped on Carnival Day, because everybody came to her house. It was open to everyone, and you don't find that any more in the modern world – which is sad.

The first year mum died, dad said to my sister, who was newly-married then, "I'm not having you do like your mother did, cutting up all that bread and making a meal for everybody" – so he booked them for lunch and tea at a restaurant, so as not to go home. Bob and I cycled into Aldeburgh and went to mother's to leave our bikes, and the gate was locked . . . and I sobbed. I was devastated! It was the first time in my life that big green gate had ever been locked against me. It really was a shock. I could not believe it.

Whenever I saw my mum she was over the stove or the sink. She used to have her hair in curlers in the mornings, and she was terribly hard-worked: but it never occurred to me I might become like her. I thought Bob was the hell of a romantic bloke – that's why he took to the arts – and I thought we would have this wonderful thing . . . but when we got married we lived up on the terrace in our cottage, and the chimney was coked up so the fire smoked, and we had a draughty kitchen with a tiny three-inch grate with hobs on each side . . . ! We got married on Saturday, and Bob was going to work on the Monday. Work was his life, and he expected me to work, just like I had always done at home or in service. Up to the time of our marriage, we would go for walks or sit in a shelter and talk about each other: but after the wedding he would have his meal, then go off sugarbeeting or doing some other job. I spent far more time with his mum than I ever did with Bob, until I decided to work alongside him.

BOB: My father was a great lover of music. I remember him having a large old gramophone with an orange horn and buying records like *The Pagan Love Song* and *Songs My Mother Used to Sing*. I used to sit in the Blaxhall Ship waiting for him, and he was like the other men – he always had his own song, *My Little Grey Home in the West*. Nobody else could sing that: it was his – and that was the same with all of them.

DORIS: My mother went to the Methodist Chapel at the top of Chopping's Hill in Aldeburgh: it was bombed during the war. They all went there on a Tuesday, and on Thursday they made curtains. The Chapel bought the material, and they paid a shilling weekly and made up their curtains and had a cup of tea together. That started at 2 and they came home at 4 p.m. and those days we had to do the fire and the washing-up because Mum was out.

Did I tell you about the hiding I got from my mother when we were newly married? We cycled home to Aldeburgh one day – this was during the war, when she had the evacuees: she gave them a lovely time and these two young lads thought the world of her. Mum was getting Sunday dinner ready when the two boys came in. I can see them now with their little shining faces, and they said: "We've brought you a present." She opened the bag and it was full of little rain-frogs all hopping about, and she was terrified. She dropped the bag and smacked them on their behinds and shouted: "Get out! Take them out with you!" That was fear, I can see, looking back, but I said to her: "You ought not to do that. It's wicked. Those poor little children are on their own, away from their parents, and you shouldn't treat them in that way." – "Don't you speak to me like that, girl!" she said: "I'm not having that from you!" – "It's not fair", I told her: "Those little boys are lonely without their parents" – and she banged my ear and knocked me right back. Bob went on eating his dinner and I felt ever so humiliated in front of my new husband, so I walked out and banged the kitchen door. "Doris, come back here!" Mother called. I wouldn't: so she said it again. "Doris! *Come . . . back . . . here!*" So I went in and she said: "Now go out that door, and shut it quietly!", and I didn't dare do otherwise. But when we were cycling home, I flew at Bob. "You're supposed to be my husband," I said, "and you didn't stand up for me!" – "No damned fear!" Bob said, "I would probably have got one, too!"

The funny thing was – when we first went together, Mum didn't like him. "You can do better for yourself than Bob," she told me, "You're not to go with him" – because he would tell me off in front of her and get really cross with me. "If he treats you like that now," she would say, "what's he going to be like when you are married? You must get someone else."

All my brothers-in-law used to think the world of Mum and buy her chocolates, but Bob would argue with her. But in the end, I can honestly say, she thought the world of him and he became one of her favourites, and if I went back home and said Bob had been on to me about something, "Serve you right!" she would say. "You are the one who stirs it up, and then you are in trouble. There's nothing wrong with *that* boy!"

BOB: I always remember the brother-in-laws, because I wasn't getting much money, and going down courting Doris I had left-offs for shoes and trousers, just something to make do with, while they had lovely suits. This was at the

22

beginning of the war. But I did have a grey pinstripe suit which I got out of the Universal Club and it cost about thirty shillings. It had begun to get tatty, so Doris said: "Let me have it at the laundry. I'll get it dyed."

DORIS: I even *paid* for it!

BOB: It came out a nice light to middle blue and it looked good until one day, cycling to Aldeburgh, the rain teemed down, and when I got there I was covered with dye – shirt and everything and all down my neck.

DORIS: The moment he arrived Bob flew at me, but Mother took my side – I really thought she was going to annihilate him!

BOB: One of my uncles was always a bit of a joker and so very dry with it. He is still alive – we saw him the other day: he'll be ninety next June. Uncle Sid – we called him C.I.D., just for a laugh – is a remarkable character and he had a very hard life – he lost two wives. He was my mother's brother, a very tall, upright man, over six foot when he was younger and went into the army.

One Christmas after he lost his first wife, he came up to Mum and Dad's in the village. We were sitting in the front room and Dad had just come back from work, because even at Christmas-time you had to go down to stoke the furnaces. There was my younger brother and myself and Doris in the front room with Sid, chatting away, when suddenly a gun-pellet came through the window with a terrific bang and Sid whipped out his handkerchief and held it over his eye and for a second we thought he had been shot, for he started crying out: "Oooh! – Oooh . . . ! – OOOH!" Father heard this from the kitchen and rushed in. "What's wrong?", he asked. "Sid's been shot in the eye!" we told him, and without any more ado off he goes to the police-station. My brother and I saw our bubble was burst and rushed off after him and told him it was all a joke. Dad was furious. He wouldn't talk to us for days afterwards, because we had made such a fool of him.

ERIC: What was it you told me once about the dance-bands at Snape?

DORIS: There were two of them – Sally Walsh, and the Miami Dance Band.

BOB: They used to tour around this area.

DORIS: Keith Cable's father, Percy, was the drummer for Sally Walsh. She used to play the violin wearing all those pearls.

BOB: There was Harry Garrod, too – he had a dance-band, but it was much smaller: they played at the sixpenny hops, Harry and his sister May on the piano. The popular tune then, in the thirties, was *Cry, Baby, Cry*, a slow foxtrot –

> *Cry, baby, cry.*
> *My eyes are dry.*
> *Cry the way*
> *You did today –*
> *You broke my heart.*

DORIS: That was in 1935 or 36, I think.

BOB: We found out that Harry took dancing lessons, so half a dozen of us lads from the village went along. He had a little room above May's 'establishment', as he called her shop, and he had a small wind-up gramophone on a chair, and we used to go round the room behind Harry, holding his shoulders and learning the steps while this gramophone was playing, and once we'd got our feet moving Harry would take the lady's part. I remember one boy – he only came twice – saying: "I won't come no more." – "Why not?" asked Harry: "You're doing well!" – "It's no good," the boy replied, "I got rhythm, but my feet ha'n't" – and he took about size twelve in boots. So he gave it up – but the rest of us learnt. Then Harry asked us to go to a sixpenny hop at Benhall or somewhere, where he showed us how to go up to the ladies and say: "Can I have the pleasure of the next dance, please?" Before that, we had just stood leaning against the gangway at the village hall: but once we learned to dance we enjoyed ourselves so much more. It was great! And Doris was a good dancer, too.

DORIS: I used to watch my father and mother. They ran the dances at the Aldeburgh Jubilee Hall for the Royal Buffs (*the Royal Ancient Order of Buffaloes*), and every Saturday night they used to make these jugs of real lemonade, sour as blazes, and I went there right up to the time I had to go into service. There was one man of about 36 who used to partner me in those early days: he taught me how to go straight and turn at the corners, and that is how I learnt really. We went to the dance one night and there was all these lovely flashing colours – not like the discos today – all these revolving lights till you felt you were in wonderland, and when we came out it was high tide and they had come to fetch us by boat. Until that moment I didn't have a clue about the floodtide, but one of the men said: "Put your arm around me and I'll lift you in the boat," and I knocked off his trilby hat and it went sailing down the street. When we got to mother's house the water was half-way up the stairs: so we had to go and live with my brother round near the school for about six weeks. Everything used to come down the Slaughden end where we lived – all the muck from the town came down there or up through the drains, and we had to have the whole house cleaned out before we could go back.

When I was younger there were two houses at Slaughden. Mrs Winter, an invalid, lived in one of them, and when there was a flood a boat had to go to her bedroom window to get her out.

BOB: We were all flooded round here. This place (*the Maltings*) was constantly being flooded, and all the barley had to be sieved out of the salt water. The river-wall used to break on the far side, the north side, not this side, and the whole village would be flooded – Snape Street, the pub (*The Crown*), all of them. That house just over the bridge here, I have seen the water up to the bedroom windows. But the village never floods nowadays, because of the break in the river-wall on this side.

DORIS: All the water comes this way now.

BOB: At the time of the spring tides in February or March, we couldn't use the road between Snape and the Maltings. We had to go round by Abbey Farm and along the railway line for four or five days until the flooding subsided.

. . . Back in the 40's and 50's every village had its own football team. They would hire a little bus – we had old Vic Foreman, from Orford – and they always changed in the pub, in the 'back'us' or kitchen, and when the game was finished, whatever the weather, we'd go into the yard and wash the mud off under the pump. I have often stood working the handle, pumping cold water on to someone. I used to finish in the engine-room at twelve on a Saturday, and at 2 p.m. I'd be standing out there on the football field in goal, the very coldest position.

When I was a boy I used to travel round with the Snape football team on Saturdays. It was one of my perks in return for cleaning all the cow muck off the field up near the garage and marking out the pitch and putting the nets up. They used to laugh because my lines weren't very straight – "Old Bob was drunk again this morning," they would say. I drove the cows into the next field, then cleaned the cow pats off so nobody would fall into them, and for that I was paid a shilling a week and allowed to travel with them free.

DORIS: Later on, when Bob played for the team, I used to go, too, and afterwards he would say: "Leave all your stuff" – so I had to wash all their white shorts and green shirts and socks, with only an oil-stove and a copper, in time for the next match.

ERIC: What did they pay you?

DORIS: Nothing! You see, Bob was their Hon. Sec.'

BOB: At the end of the war we had a field, but we hadn't any gear, so we bought some goal posts from a team that had been disbanded, but then we needed nets and shirts and everything, so one day we had a General Meeting and Doris came, and she went right home afterwards and unbeknown to any of us she wrote to the *Daily Mirror* and asked for what they called her *Secret Wish* – a set of football shirts.

DORIS: I told them my son and my husband both played for the same team, and I still have the poster that was put up in the village – "*Snape Woman Granted Secret Wish*". We had a committee meeting to choose the colours, and they were Bukta shirts – really good stuff.

BOB: Everybody was thrilled and the first match we played was in the Leiston League and Doris was invited to kick off, and that got us into trouble with the secretary who said we should have consulted him-because, after all, she might have scored!

DORIS: So after that I had the privilege of washing all their shorts and shirts!

BOB: We had a supporters' club which gave concerts and socials and so on-it was a great interest in those days when nobody had television. And I made a wheel – a Wheel of Fortune. I got a bicycle wheel and mounted it on a big sheet of hardboard and coloured it all round where the spokes were, and I painted numbers from 1 to 12, and there was an arrow which went round when the wheel was twisted. According to which number the arrow stopped at, people got a card for a packet of cigarettes or something like that, but I always planned things so the club would get fifty per cent profit. Sometimes we made twenty or thirty pounds in one evening. We used to have little fetes, too, on the Crown meadow, with bowling for the pig . . .

DORIS: I was on the jumble stall.

BOB: At first we had skittles up a plank – the distance up the plank was about eighteen feet and the skittles were set on a triangle at the top, but some of the chaps who came along were professionals. They would arrive early in the afternoon and aim the bowls at terrific speed and knock all the skittles down, and when that had happened three times nobody else could play because they had won the pig. They spoilt it for everybody else.

So after a couple of seasons, I got a board and cut holes all along it, then I found some polo-balls – and the higher the number of the hole, the less space I allowed for the balls to go through. I used to walk round the sports grounds and find the most uneven bit of ground and rig the board up there. So invariably some young kid would score a number eight just by luck and he would get the pig – and the professionals would come along, look, then go away again. Mr Hurren, down at Dunningworth Hall, gave us a pig every year and we would have it squeaking and running round inside a wall of straw bales.

We had a greasy pig, too – you chased that right around the sports field, but every time you caught it, it would slip out of your hands. At the swimming club, we had greasy poles in the river, too – a big pole in the middle covered with grease and you sat astride it and had pillow fights. You would be holding on tight, but suddenly down you'd go into the water – that was great fun!

DORIS: All those years ago there was something special about making our own pleasures . . .

5

"A terrible thing happened"

ERIC: Bob, you didn't tell us what you did in the Navy. You were in small boats, weren't you?

BOB: I was in minesweepers – they were trawlers, wooden or metal fishing-boats from Lowestoft or Hull. Deep sea fishers they were; until the war most of them fished off Iceland. First of all I went to the *Ganges* in 1941 for my training. There was a base for minesweepers up at Lowestoft, but I couldn't get on one of those; so I transferred from what Doris's mum called the 'real' Navy . .

DORIS: My brother Kenneth was on the Arethusa and he was drifting in a minefield for three days, and that was a terrible time and my mum was ever so worried, and I said "I worry, too, about Bob," and my mother said "Don't be stupid, Doris! Your brother Ken is in the *real* Navy – not like Bob" – and Bob was sweeping mines!

BOB: I joined the Royal Naval Patrol Service at the *HMS Europa* at Lowestoft. When I went down there, I slept on the stage of the concert hall, the *Sparrow's Nest*. We had coke stoves which had to be stoked all through the night, and they gave us each two blankets and we slept on the floor, and it was so perishing cold and draughty and the fumes from the coke were so bad we all wanted to get a ship and move out of it. I remember hitch-hiking down to Snape to see Doris and not getting a lift. As I walked south through Pakefield, the sirens went and I trudged on and on, and one or two cars and lorries passed but not one of them picked me up, and I walked on until I got to Saxmundham – 21 miles – and my feet were so sore! When I got to Sax, I borrowed a bicycle from Doris's brother Billy.

DORIS: He woke me up in the middle of the night. I opened the window and called out "Who's there? – "Who the hell do you think?", Bob said: "Hitler?" He had to go back next morning.

BOB: I had been drafted to Scotland, and I knew Doris would be worried to death if she didn't hear. I was sent up to Leith, and that was my first minesweeper, operating from Edinburgh. I had never been to sea before and I was terribly sea-sick my first trip. That was on the *Brabant* and we were mine-sweeping up around May Island and on to Iceland – terribly cold. Those ships have a paravane which is more like a torpedo, and you tow that aft of amidships. There are four sweepers working together, and they take turns in being flotilla-leader, which is the position of danger. There is more or less a ton of wire which is towed like a fishing net: it is very tight and weighted down by doors or 'gates', one down in the water near the ship, the other probably a hundred yards astern, and you have to watch the paravane, the big torpedo with a flag on, all the time, because if the flag went down you knew you had got a mine. When you 'swept' the mine, you broke the moorings and it bobbed up to the surface and you had to shoot it. Sometimes it was really very difficult to sink one, what with the rise and fall of the ship and the bobbing up and down of the mine itself. One day we had a terrible experience when we pulled in the sweep and there was a mine hooked up in the 'gate': we pulled it right alongside, then pushed it off with boat-hooks . . . But we didn't really worry too much. I think if I had been older, I would have done.

DORIS: You never have worried about anything!

BOB: I was minesweeping all through the war, and I did a few Russian convoys in an armed trawler, and then came D Day. When you were on convoys you didn't go into harbour – you waited outside to collect your ships. One day down at Falmouth we almost got blasted out of the water, because the Germans used to come over in those old Stukas which shrieked as they dived down, and the noise was almost more terrifying than the bombs, though we'd got ships armed with pom-poms and anti-aircraft guns. The real trouble was, while we

Doris, Bob and baby Stephen, 1943

were blazing away at the Stukas, the E boats would come racing in, and before you knew what was happening, they would be hitting you below the belt. They were so fast, and they used to tie up behind buoys. We didn't have radar: we had what they called ASDIC *(an echo-sounding device to detect submarines)*. You'd pick up something on the screen, but when you looked on the chart you'd find it marked there as a buoy: so you were completely unprepared.

The last few months before demob, I was coxswain of a TSRB *(Torpedo Safety Recovery Boat)*. We used to go out and hang around waiting for flying-boats from the Fleet Air Arm base at Macrihanish *(near Campbelltown)* to come in to land, because sometimes they turned them over and then we had to cut the crew out of them.

DORIS: You can tell how little we knew about names in those days because one morning Bob came home – I was making the bed – and he called up the stairs: "I've just come to tell you I'm moving again." – "Where to?", I asked. – "To Macrihanish." – "I don't want you to go to India!", I said.

BOB: While I was on the TSRB's a terrible thing happened. We had to go over to Londonderry – a dreadful rough trip through the Irish Sea. We had fire-extinguishers on board, like all ships of that size, but the foam one broke away from its bulkhead and the glass smashed. Next night we had a fire on board – the whole messdeck caught fire. There was a paraffin-heater and the lads had let paraffin run under the matting until it was saturated, and somehow it got afire. We tried to get the matting up on deck and the whole wheelhouse caught fire – it was made of Perspex. So there we were on fire from stem to stern in Campbelltown harbour. The trouble was, my mate on the boat next to us had gone ashore, asking me to look after his boat. All his crew had gone: so when I knew we couldn't do anything with our boat, I told one of the lads to go to where they had fire-alarms on the jetty, then I jumped across to the other boat, broke into the wheel-house and got the engine going – so we saved one of them. The only extinguisher on my boat was a Pyrene for electrical fires, and when I used that we were just about gassed. So my boat was burnt out: but those Perkins diesel engines were terrific: when we tried them a few days later they started up at once, although the boat had been full of water. But we lost everything we had . . . They were selling off those boats about then for £100, without the engines: they took those out. As houseboats they would hold four or five people.

DORIS: I bet they put those engines in a shed and forgot about them!

BOB: Oh, yes! Typical Navy . . . ! The most frightened I ever got during the war, and I was terrified then, we were down in Dover harbour. We had been towing barges backwards and forwards along the coast and it was just before D-Day: there were about fifty trawlers involved, and the whole thing was a gimmick to confuse the enemy. We were using the outer channel some ten miles out, and we lost several trawlers because it was so easy to pick them off, but it wasn't too bad until one day we called in at Dover harbour and got dive-bombed. The deck was all split open in front of us – that was the Stukas – and they were shelling us as well. There was always shelling at Dover, either by them or by us.

I ended up, as I told you, in the TSRB's up at Macrihanish. That was nice, really. I got Doris up there and we were all saying "Roll on, demob!" – but when it came, we wondered what it was all about. Then it was straight back to the Maltings: I didn't even give myself a holiday. Five years I had been away, and they had had different people through my engine room. Of course, I had to go up to Lowestoft to get my demob suit.

DORIS: My sister married a chap from Worcester, and mother said: "Bob will be best man, 'cos he's the only one with a new suit."

BOB: I saw Cyril Smythe, the manager of the Maltings, and said I wanted my job back and I went into the engine-room, doing the crystal malt.

ERIC: Doris, you promised to tell me about the time you were up at Tarbert in Argyll and your younger boy was badly scalded.

DORIS: I was up there with the boys in a furnished room . . .

BOB: By this time the war had finished. It was 1946 and I was in the TSRB's, waiting to be demobbed.

DORIS: What happened was, for boiling water I had a trivet over the fire, and the baby was in bed asleep – he was about six months then – and the landlady, who was ever so nice, had called me through because it was my birthday and she had bought me two pillowcases with little embroidered flowers on the tops, and I sat on the edge of her bed chatting, and I was happy because of my birthday, when suddenly there was this awful scream, and we ran through, and the landlady's boy had taken Tony the baby off the bed on to the rug – to play, I suppose, and I had put a saucepan of water on to boil to wash up the breakfast things and the boy went to pick it up, but the handle was so hot he dropped it all over the baby's back and neck. He was very badly scalded. Even now he has terrible scars.

BOB: Doris fetched me from the ship – I ran the whole way up to where she was staying – and my first sight of Tony, he looked like a rabbit that had just been skinned.

DORIS: They kept him in Tarbert for three days and the doctor said: "Medically there is nothing can be done: it's only with the Lord . . ." He was a very religious man, I expect. But then poison set in. So they took him to the York Hill Children's Hospital outside Glasgow. The Soldiers', Sailors' and Airmen's Association paid for a car to take us, and he was about four flights up in the hospital – but even in the road we could hear his screams when they put him in a saline bath – it was dreadful!

BOB: We were over a hundred miles from Glasgow, where the hospital was.

DORIS: Bob used to travel from Tarbert by bus to see him.

BOB: When the bus reached Glasgow I only just had time to get a tram up to the hospital, see Tony for ten minutes or so, then rush down to catch the bus back to Tarbert.

ERIC: Wasn't there anybody to help you?

DORIS: No. We didn't know anybody up there.

BOB: We were on our own. Going to Glasgow was like going from here to London and having to come straight back, and since it was a local bus it stopped at every little place.

DORIS: The day Tony should have come out, Bob had been demobbed and we were all excited – Bob and my elder boy Stephen and me – because we were going to fetch him, then travel back home, but I woke about six that morning crying my eyes out, and I said to Bob: "I've had an awful nightmare. I've been pulling Tony back from the dead all night long. He's got scarlet fever and he's covered in spots." The landlady was very kind. She brought me a cup of cocoa (I don't know why cocoa) and said: "It's just the excitement, because you are going home." – "I feel awful", I told her: "I've been pulling him back the whole night long."

Bob told me not to talk rubbish – it was just a bad dream: but at nine that morning we had a telegram to say: 'Your boy has measles. On danger list. Come at once.' Somebody had taken a baby into the hospital with measles, and Tony was so ill he caught it, and they'd put this skin-graft on him but it would not take, then another one, then a third: so it was going to be a very long wait, and they told us: "You'd better go home. There's nothing you can do here, and he doesn't even know you", because he was only a baby and he had already been in there three months; and they told us they would send for us whichever way it happened. So we came home to Snape and we were back here another three months before we could fetch Tony home again.

He was very accident-prone, our Tony. There was a lady from Iken some time later who used to come and sell us eggs. Tony had a feeding bottle, a medicine bottle with a teat, because we didn't have plastic in those days. "I've always liked these cottages on the terrace", the lady said: so I asked her in to look round, and Tony followed us upstairs, then fell down and cut his eye badly – his face was one mass of blood. Dr Ryder Richardson, who was always full of fun, said: "Well, if he's ever knocked down in an accident, there'll be no problem about marks of identification!"

6

"We knew how happy we were"

BOB: It was 1938, the time of Neville Chamberlain, when Doris and I first met (in fact, we had a discussion about that on Aldeburgh beach), late 1938, and that was when I started work down here at the Maltings. My father worked here all his life apart from when he was a prisoner-of-war in the 1914-18 war: my grandfather worked here, and my great-grandfather. I started work in this very room (*the big room of their ground-floor flat looking across the marshes towards Iken*). This was a turning-bay. I worked on the top floor. I started as one of the day-gang – they always put you in the day-gang to begin with – and they gave me a truck of coke to empty and I got threepence extra for that. Two of us on the job shared sixpence, the *old* sixpence, extra above our pay, and that was marvellous. We were then getting about thirty six shillings a week. I was fifteen, and I got the same money as my dad, because we did the same work. They didn't mind, boy or man, so long as you were strong. When you came down here, you were a man.

My job was turning the barley to help it to germinate. The grain was soaked, then spread out on concrete bays where you kept it at about 70 degrees (if the temperature went higher, you had to spread it thinner), and gradually it grew.

After about eight days it was all clammy, roots and grain, and then it was loaded into the kiln area to be dried off. It was a constant process – emptying out your 'steep' after what we called 'wetting'. 'Wet ho!' they used to call, and we'd all

Bob, Doris, Stephen and Tony, Iken 1947

go in next door where the music-school is now and throw the barley down the spout into the 'steep' where it was soaked for a couple of days – no, three days – and then the water was drained away and the barley thrown out – 'Empty!', they would call, and all the men would go in to empty the 'steeps'. Then, as well as turning the moist grain on the floors, you had the grain in the kilns to turn and the furnaces to stoke up, and there would be another 'steep' to empty next day – you never stopped. There were four drying kilns in there where the concert-hall is now, with eight large furnaces underneath.

DORIS: We lived up on the terrace in Snape after the war. Bob worked from 6 a.m. to 2 p.m. at the Maltings, and then – because the pay was so low – he and his mates would rush home, get a meal, and hurry off to another job. He used to wave his sweat-rag outside the kiln door (*now the concert-hall door*), and I would be looking out and I'd dish his meal up ready for the moment he got home, then off he would go hoeing sugarbeet or some other job. I had to hoe and pull sugarbeet, too, when I first got married, in the old-fashioned way.

BOB: When I started work at fifteen, I had to learn how to carry a coomb of malt – twelve stone: that was my O-levels. For my A-levels, I had to carry a coomb of *barley* – sixteen stone. You had to learn how to carry them up a plank into a truck and how to spring with the plank: you had to get it nicely balanced on your shoulders and that helped you to walk. You had to be really strong. Before coming down here, I worked for Sir Guy Hambling, Margot Hare's father, up at the Hall Farm in Snape. I plucked all the chickens for Margot's wedding up in London – about 120 of them: each guest had a little chicken on his plate.

The important thing in malting was keeping the 'pieces', as we called them, level, so that the temperature was the same all over: there were glasses – temperature-glasses – stuck in the grain, and the manager and the assistant-manager would mark the temperatures up on a plan on the wall, with T meaning Turn, D for Drag, S for Stick-plough, L for Leave. For getting the barley from the turning-bay to the floor of the kilns, we used barrows without wheels – long wooden barrows with handles at both ends. When you wanted to move your 'piece' further on, you used a can of water to wet the concrete so your barrow would slide. Then you filled the barrow, got down and lifted that tremendous weight with your shoulder, then pushed – and then you tipped it out. The same barrows were used for emptying the kilns. The malt came up the elevators (we *did* have elevators), and there would be four men barrowing the malt onto the elevator down below, and three men up above in the kiln emptying the malt down the spouts.

John Braithwaite, when he was finishing off this flat, had a lot of photos of the men who worked here, like those framed enlargements in the downstairs corridor of the concert-hall, and he got a whole set done for me. There was one man, John Whiting, lived next door to us along Hell's Row (that's what they called Church Road) at Snape where my family had moved to by the beginning of the war. He was about eighty and badly crippled, and we had an air-raid shelter up the garden, a hole in the earth with a sheet of galvanised iron on top, and since I was the only youngster along our row, I used to carry John up there on my shoulder and put the poor old devil down in the hole. The picture of him I have got was taken in 1890, when he was about thirty.

There were three boys and a girl in my family, and we had a garden and an allotment. Our garden in Snape was about ten rod, a massive piece of land, as wide as this flat and about a hundred yards long, and we had to dig it all.

DORIS: That was Bob's idea of a good time when we were courting. I had to come down to the allotments to pick the potatoes up and do the sprouts. It was Bob's father's garden, but *I* still had to do it!

But oh! you ought to have known the devastation here when the Maltings shut down in 1965! We were lucky because we knew how happy we were (though obviously the men had to work hard) – we knew, and sometimes you don't until you're left, do you? The men used to cycle up as you were going to Millie Lomax or any of the shops, and 'Hallo, Doris!' they would say and get off to talk to you. Then Bob would come home and he'd say: 'Coo! there's a rum bit of scandal today!' Well, you couldn't wait till next day to hear the rest of the story.

BOB: We ran the Football Club from down here, picked the team and had our committee meetings, and the Bowls Club, the Tennis Club and the Swimming Club, and concert-parties as well – all from the Maltings.

DORIS: I was Prince Charming at one concert . . .

BOB: We did a pantomime in rhyme for Nicky Nicholson: "*The fairy godmamma, Hurra, hurra, hurra!*", and all sorts of things like that in aid of the Football Club. My sister-in-law Lil was a good singer, still is, and Claud Hart was here (he died about 1965) – he was a terrific singer and entertainer, a marvellous man. He used to do "*Father Jones went up the aisle, hickety-hick, hickety-hick . . !*", and that sort of stuff. Us two used to get together and do silly little turns like the old Log Cabin, where he would be cooking away on the stove we'd made, and I was the son who came in: this was a filler-in really, to pass time during the concert until somebody else came on, so we used to drag it out. I'd be munching an apple and he'd be stirring the pot on the stove. "Where's your pa, son?"- and after munching some apple and walking up and down I'd say, "In the barn, ma." – "What's he doing there?" – "Hanging from a beam, ma." Another long silence, and then, "Did you cut him down, son?" – "No, ma." – "Why not, son?" Another bite of apple, another long silence, then, "Cos he ain't dead yet, ma."

We did lots of things like that. You'd walk on stage with this big handkerchief round your neck and a lipstick mark across your throat, and Claud would say, "Bob, what's up, boy? You look as miserable as someone who has just cut his throat!" – and you'd pull the handkerchief off and say, "I have . . . !"

DORIS: (*laughing*) Very invigorating stuff! We probably enjoyed it more than the audience.

BOB: And all this used to be arranged down here at the Maltings. Everything happened here, even the gossip started down here. It was the hub of the village.

DORIS: An American friend of ours lived round Gromford and he said once: "You're having a concert? I'll sing for you." Well, we were worried out of our lives, because we were professionals . . .

BOB: I told Claud: "Old Jim Eastep, he's going to give us a song." – "Who the hell is he?", Claud asked. So I told him, "He's this Yank lives over at Stone Cottage." "Is he any good?", Claud asked. "He might be a let-down. Is he coming to a rehearsal, same as we do?" – "No", I said, and I thought "God! I hope he doesn't let us down." But Jim turned up and he got on stage and he had a terrific voice . . .

DORIS: He'd only won the All-Europe contest for the American Air Force Singers!

Doris and Bob (in his demob suit), Clacton 1950

BOB: He sang *Autumn Leaves* and songs like that, and they wouldn't let him go. After that we went on and they all called out "You pack it up!" He was just too good for us.

DORIS: He was fantastic – and he still writes to us. We've even had invitations to his children's weddings and they were babies when they left here . . .

But going back to the Maltings . . . One breakfast-time Bob came home and he said, "I can't make it out. We have all got to meet on the floor at eleven this morning. I reckon we are going to get a rise or an extra day's holiday", and he was that excited . . .

BOB: 1965 it was – over twenty years ago . . .

DORIS: When he came home, I asked 'Well, what is it?", and he said, "We're going into liquidation", and that was just like . . .

BOB: Like the end of the world for our little community. We didn't know anything else-we hadn't worked anywhere else.

DORIS: Bob got a job painting, at Smythe's, but because we had always been together – well, he went at seven in the morning and he didn't come home till about six, and to us that was terrible, and he was unhappy because if he finished at four he had to look like work until five – not like here where you could come home when you were finished. So he didn't stop long, although they were sorry to lose him.

BOB: It was a totally different life. Here, we were like in a cloister – as we are now, I suppose.

DORIS: We weren't ready for the outside world: we didn't need it, to be truthful.

BOB: The whole thing dissolved. Everyone had to finish by August, and all the houses were sold, twenty or more of them, and the pub, *The Plough and Sail* – sold quite cheaply.

DORIS: I often think of it with a smile because a couple of friends of ours said, "How can you stay on in this rut?" When it is summertime, I often wish they would come back and see the 'rut' we are in. I am ever so glad the concert hall was built. We have been so lucky, because we knew the Maltings as it used to be, and then we saw the concert hall, then the music school with its own premises, and then we had two years of the Sizewell Enquiry, plus weddings, and each year the antiques fair – and still it is this old building come back to what it was. Sometimes we wake up at five in the morning and Bob will say, "Heck if I know – but there's father clomping about, coming to work!"

BOB: The room where we sleep is where they emptied the barley from the 'steep' and I can remember it with the barley and the water in it, and you'd go there first thing in the morning and the rats would run all over and up the beams to get out of the way, hundreds of them, because there was food and drink for them here and warmth.

DORIS: When that building (*the present music-school*) was still old and we slept here, two or three winters Bob used to have a broom and bang on the ceiling to

"We are redundant" – closure of the Maltings 1965

get rid of the rats up above. They sounded as if they had hob-nailed boots on. We heard the horses, too . . .

BOB: They used to have Suffolk punches to shunt the trucks, up to the mid-fifties, and there was always a pony to bring coke up to the engine room. There are two types of malt, you see – pale malt and crystal malt, and the crystal malt is cylinder-dried over coke fires. The pale malt is dried in kilns – but the crystal is dried much quicker. They use it for foodstuffs like Ovaltine and for very dark beer like stout.

DORIS: (*To Bob*) When you were in the engine-room, you were thin . . .

BOB: Hard work that was . . . heat and sweat.

DORIS: More money, though!

BOB: You had to stoke your furnaces and slice them. They were on rails: you pushed them along with your feet, so you could take the slides off the cylinders and tip the malt out, then re-load them – then you put the slides back and moved the furnaces under again. It was quite a skilful job testing the malt. You had a long spoon and you pushed it into the cylinder and got some malt on the palm of your hand and you could more or less tell by the colour whether it was cooked. There were five sacks in each cylinder and it took roughly an hour and a half to cook: two of us were in charge of the four cylinders of crystal malt. The other kind, the pale malt, took four days in the kiln. It looked like a tropical forest when the wet barley was giving off all its dampness – it was terrible! With four of you in a row turning the grain you couldn't see each other. Everything was soaking wet and you could see steam coming out of the 'bluffers' or chimneys.

DORIS: You got pneumonia three times.

BOB: It was football did that, going from a hot place like the engine-room or a turning-kiln with temperatures up to the skies, then standing about on a football-pitch this time of year (*November*). I used to keep goal . . .

DORIS: When he got pneumonia it was terrible. I had to go to work on account of the money (I worked for Mrs Irving for sixteen years), and I would come home and change his wet sheets and he kept saying about this hole in his head and would I fill it up . . . ?

7

"Look at the character in those faces"

BOB *(looking at old photographs)*: These are men that worked down here from the 1890s. I bet they stood a long time to have their photographs taken. That young lad, *(1)* the apprentice carpenter, is Alfred Andrews. He lived in Wink's House (it was named after his successor), across from the Maltings. That was always the carpenter's house, a semi-detached. I remember Alfred just after the outbreak of war when he was nearly 70, close on retiring age.

DORIS: Even in those days, with no washing machines, look at the pure white of his shirt and apron. And his bow-tie!

BOB: That one *(2)* is Tom Savage. He is holding a 'turner' – not a shovel, but a flat-edged wooden tool like a spade made on the premises by the carpenters. They made all the tools, and the men used to burn their names on the backs and sometimes designs of chickens or pigs. Tom Savage was a foreman maltster. He is holding the 'cot' (the handle) of his 'turner'. When you were turning the soaked grain, you had to do it 'both hands afore' – that is to say, you walked to the right across your 'piece' of grain turning it, then you changed hands for the return journey to your left. It is very difficult until you get used to it – like getting off a bicycle both ways.

You can see what we called 'lijahs' round his trousers below the knee. Those were straps or strings to stop the mice running up inside his legs, because

43

1. Alfred Andrews
Apprentice carpenter

2. Tom Savage
Foreman Maltster

3. 'Spider' Alexander
Kiln Worker

4. Harry Puttock
Gardener

5. J. Smith
Horseman and Shunter

6. John Whiting
Roaster (Kiln Worker)

7. A. Andrews
Carpenter

8. Assistant Bricklayer
to J. Sparrow

there were hundreds of mice and rats. The next (3) is Spider Alexander, a kiln worker.

DORIS: Look at the character in those faces!

BOB: He is making lime-mortar by burning lime in a kiln. I remember him as a very old man, but it says here he was a 'junior' in 1896. He was a rather wicked old man. My brother used to deliver milk at the beginning of the war, and he would give the old age pensioners a touch extra – just top up their jugs as he ladled the milk from the churn, until this old man wrote to the farmer saying he didn't want 'charity'. He nearly got my brother the sack.

BOB: Harry Puttock (4) – he was a gardener, like Alfred Andrews in his waistcoat with lapels and his bow-tie . . .

DORIS: That's not a Suffolk name! He's a real grandad-looking man.

BOB: J. Smith, *'Horseman and shunter'* (5) – and just look at the darns in his trousers. He lost his arm between the buffers of two trucks. That was when they had Suffolk punches, three of them, for the shunting.

DORIS: He's got a white bow-tie. It's incredible! *They* wear them in the morning, and we wear them at night!

BOB: Now (6) it's John Whiting. He's the old man – I told you – I used to carry to the air-raid shelter. He has got his 'Spoon', look, for dipping in the cylinders and taking samples of malt; they were about eight foot long, so you didn't get too badly burned. Our hands used to be completely stained brown from doing that.

My grandfather was foreman in the crystal end of the malting when a Mr Cowell was managing director, and the men got around Sam, my grandfather, to see him about some extra money. They wanted more pay and less work: so the poor old boy went along and he was so overcome when he got there he put it the wrong way round and asked Mr Cowell for 'more work and less pay', and Mr Cowell answered: "Right, Sam, we'll see what we do for you!" But they did get a little extra all the same.

That one (7) is Alfred Andrew's father – carpenter: and the next one (8) was *'Assistant to J. Sparrow'*: one of his two daughters was my teacher in the Infants' School at Blaxhall. You see those aprons they are wearing? They are made from sacks. When I first came to the Maltings, we had sacking-boots: none of us had water-boots. You cut a square of sacking and folded it a special way round your feet and tied it with string, and when you went in the 'steep' the water didn't come through. They got damp, but not soaking wet, so we would hang them up to dry, then use them again.

ERIC: Why did they need two tilers and bricklayers?

BOB: They had nine houses up in the village, they had *The Plough and Sail*, plus six houses at the top, Hillside Cottages, and three more semi-detached, and the Station House, and a few the other side of the road, and the offices here – and they did a lot of furnace-work because all the furnaces had to be rebricked at the end of the season.

This photo (9) of the fire-brigade in their brass helmets – they worked at the Maltings and I knew all of them, but I don't know if any of them is still alive.

9. The Maltings Fire Brigade, c. 1933. Left to right: Alfred Davidson, Percy Ship, Wiggy Felgate, Dumpling Hudson, Jimmy Rumsey, Sid Messenger, Ernie Burrows, Bony Bloomfield, Tom Haggar, Stanley Haggar.

10. Annual outing to Yarmouth, 1919. Left to right, standing: John Taylor, Bony Bloomfield, unknown, Dumpling Hudson, two unknowns, Philip Jay, Jimmy Foreman, Grandfather Sam Ling, Druddy Ling. Seated: Harold Smith, Willy Mayhew, unknown, Mr Ship, Jolly Fred Howell, Pimple Six Foot Osborne.

This big picture (*10*) is of the annual outing in 1915, but many of these must have been away at the war by then. That's Uncle Druddy, Esau's boy – Esau was my father's brother. That little man was Pimple Six-Foot Osborne: he was a barge-skipper actually, not quite five foot tall. That one, Jolly Fred, never smiled in his life. That's Yorkie Mayhew – and little Wallie, who worked where the Music School is now – a very comical little man: he used to say he was tall until he came down here and hit his head so often on the beams! And Porkie John Taylor, our dear neighbour, a marvellous man – he brought up two girls and a boy, and he should have had a medal as big as a frying-pan; one of the kindest men I ever met. And Bony Bloomfield, the tall one there – and Dumpling Hudson – and Harold – he is still alive.

We used to go on outings every year to Yarmouth in those old charabancs like the one they are sitting in. They put the crates of beer in the boot, and

I suppose the first stop would be Kelsale to have a drink, and when they got to Yarmouth they would go to a pub called *The Divers*, where they could sing and tap-dance and they would spend the whole day there. They never went to the beach or anywhere like that, but when they came home at night they had had a lovely day and my dad would be drunk as a lord and he'd brought mum another alarm-clock and he would come in with it ringing away.

DORIS: Bob's uncle was saying last Sunday how like his mother Bob is, and you can see he's got the same high cheekbones as his grandfather has in this charabanc picture, almost gypsy-looking. He's got a lot of reserve, like his mother had. Why I think a lot of Bob is because you can't get at him, not right at the core of him, even though you live with him a long while, and his mother was the same.

BOB: I used to go and eat my grandfather's dinner every Sunday: he would come home from *The Plough* three parts cut, so I helped him out, and after he would clap his hands together and shout: "That was a lovely dinner, dear!", although I had eaten nearly all of it. My grandmother came from Yorkshire. I remember her always wearing a peaked cap and smoking Player's cigarettes – she kept a packet on the mantelpiece above the fire, and they used to have those long glass tubes over the mantelpiece, going up to short ones at the top.

DORIS: Everybody had them – green or dark blue, long at the bottom, short at the top. (*These were decorative rolling-pins*).

That one shows my dad when he got a gold watch for working all those years at the tennis courts in Aldeburgh. I take after my dad for meetings, because I was on Snape Parish Council for eleven years – there were eleven men and me, but I gave it up when I was sixty. And this is Mrs Irving's house at the Wadd in Gromford, where I worked for sixteen years.

BOB: This one is my Uncle Dick. He was courting my aunt May and they went over to Blaxhall to see my grandfather, who was king of the castle in his own house. Dick was a very short man – Dick Smy, from Orford – but my aunt was proud of him, so she took him in and said, "Father, this is Dick Smy." – "Oh! so you are Dick Smy, are you?" – "Yes, Mr Ling, but they call me 'Biff'" – "You'll do no biffing here! I do all the biffing in this house!", the old man told him. So poor Dick was cut down to size.

Dick was a cowman, and I used to be lent out to them for the summer holidays. He worked at Dunningworth Hall, near Snape Bridge, until the farmer, MacShane (there were lots of Scotsmen in this area) moved to Wickford in Essex and they went with him. It was all hand-milking in those days, and I remember going to see Dick in the nettus (neat-house) when he was milking, and he could turn the cow's teat up and squirt you right in the face with it. He was a dabster for jokes like that. I used to be well looked-after at Wickford – plenty of milk to drink and plenty of food – but Aunt May was terribly cruel . . .

DORIS: She didn't have any children.

BOB: She would get me to stand on a chair and sing, and if I didn't I would get a thrashing. Several times she knocked me down – but I liked working on the farm and riding the horses back from the harvest-fields. They fed me well – but if I didn't eat it all, I would get another thrashing.

Doris's father, 'Woffy' –
William Oliver Fyrer, 1936

Bob's uncle Dick – 'Biff' Smy –
and Aunt May

8

"When we were gravediggers"

ERIC: How was it, when the Maltings shut down in 1965, you got the idea of gravedigging?

BOB: I used to dig a few graves round here, part-time. I had done that for about five years at Snape and Friston and other places, because finishing at the Maltings at two each afternoon I could do other work. I always remember the first grave I dug, up at Snape churchyard – I had terrible nightmares. I still have, not nightmares now but dreams – not fears about the grave or being in it, but fears of not getting it finished in time, because gravedigging has to be so exact. You can't still be digging the hole when the cortege is coming: it has got to be done – and the dream I very often have nowadays I've got about four graves to dig and I have left myself from half past twelve to two o'clock to do them in, which is impossible!

DORIS: It took us thirteen hours to do one once – that was at Coddenham . . .

BOB: That was in the hot summer and we were digging through chalk.

DORIS: I was wheelbarrowing pails of water about a hundred yards along the road to pour in the grave.

BOB: The strange thing was, we had dug a grave there before and that was quite sandy, but there was a seam of chalk ran through the churchyard. The

Rushmere churchyard 1967

trouble was, there is a cemetery at Coddenham opposite the church and I misread the letter. We should have dug the grave *by* the church, but we did it in the cemetery, so we gave ourselves a terrific lot of work. It was the hardest grave we had ever dug – middle of summer, the ground all dried up, and hard chalk . . .

DORIS: That was for three, too – a treble grave, for daughter, husband and father . . .

BOB: About nine feet deep.

DORIS: In the end Bob was so exhausted he got a hammer and chisel, and while he chiselled away I was getting out buckets of crumbs: and we sat shaking because we thought we would never get it done . . .

BOB: All the way down you could see where my fork had been chipping bits out.

DORIS: Another time we went to a village near Ipswich to reopen a grave and we felt ashamed because it only took about three-quarters of an hour: so we got it ready, and as we went back through the village they asked: "Been to take a look at your place, then?" – "Yes", we said, because we knew them all and we didn't want them to think we had already done it.

I'll never forget once, though! I never knew if Bob was a brave man or a damned fool – I never *did* know – but he had to dig at a convent along the Woodbridge Road near Ipswich, and for lack of room we had to dig four deep. Bob was down there on a ladder, and when a train went past below the churchyard you could feel the whole ground shaking, and I said: "Bob, for goodness sake, board the sides up" – but we had only got enough boards to go part way, and I said: "The earth will fall in." – "Hold that ladder still", he said, "If I hear the earth go, I'll run up." Do you know, we no sooner got home that there was a phone-call from the undertaker. Not only had the sides caved in but the boards had snapped in two – and Bob could have been down there. *I* could see the danger, but either he couldn't see it or he wanted to finish the job.

BOB: The whole thing started when I got a call one evening from Bob Reid, the son of a chap I used to work with at the Maltings. He had gone into the funeral business, first with Ashford's in Saxmundham, then with the Ipswich Co-op. He knew that I used to dig a few graves: so as their Ipswich man was finishing, he was too old, he offered me a job with the Co-op. I told him I didn't want to work weekly but I wouldn't mind contracting. We went up to see them and it was agreed I would give them priority. At that time we had just bought our house on Snape Terrace and the one next door, which had belonged to old John Taylor, a lovely old neighbour of ours: when he died, we bought them both, and we were in the middle of renovating them. I would be doing a bit of bricklaying, and Doris would come out to say there had been a phone-call . . .

DORIS: We always worked together . . .

BOB: I bought an eight foot Commer van. The roof was glass, and we used to laugh because when we drove under the bridge at Needham Market I used to duck down like this . . . At that time we used to dig all round Stowmarket, Stoke-by-Nayland, even as far as the Shotley peninsula, Trimley, and Felixstowe. They offered us a lovely flat at Ipswich because they just couldn't find another gravedigger, but we didn't take it because we loved Snape.

Lots of churches we used to go to in those days the Parson would give us the key so we could get out the Burial Book and find out where the graves were, in case we had to re-open one.

DORIS: They got to know us ever so well!

ERIC: What did you tell me once about the rector and the oyster soup?

DORIS: This American gave me a tin of oysters and I didn't know what the deuce to do with them, and I hate waste, so I thought, I'll make some soup. So I got some potatoes and onions and boiled it all up and it smelt lovely, and when we were over at Whitton Church we were having our dinner and the rector there – he was ever so nice and always stopped to talk to us – "Cor!", said he, "That's a nice smell. What have you got there?" – "Oyster soup", I told him, "Would you like some?" – "No", he said, "I haven't got time for that – but where are the old-time gravediggers with their penknives and their bread, cheese and onion? You sit here eating oyster soup; so how much money do you get?" He still laughs about that now, when we see him.

ERIC: I wanted to ask you about leaving the barrow at Coddenham.

DORIS: It was part of my job always to take the boards back to the church and collect up the green mats and put them in the back of the van while Bob was finishing off. This day he was in a terrible hurry because we had to go to Shotley, twelve or fifteen miles away; so he asked – "Right?" – "Right!", I told him, and hopped in the van – and when we were driving through Ipswich, which was terribly crowded with traffic, he asked, "You did get everything?" – and then I suddenly realised the barrow wasn't there. "Where *did* you put it?" – "I left it in the middle of the road." So when we came to a roundabout we turned round and drove all the way back and when we reached Coddenham there was the wheelbarrow still standing in the middle of the road and all the cars going round it. Nobody had moved it.

One day we went early to a church and that was the first time I ever realised what a lonely time policemen have. We were so busy we went to dig this grave in the early hours of the morning. "We can do it by the lights of the van", Bob said – and we were digging away, chatting, when suddenly we heard a voice. "Who's there?" – "That's *us*", I said. – "Who's 'us'?" – "The gravediggers." – "Thank God! For a moment I thought it was witchcraft" – because at that time there was a lot of talk about witchcraft. I thought to myself then, that's not a very nice job being in a lonely place like that churchyard on your own. He seemed really pleased when he found out who we were.

BOB: When we were gravedigging I had a letter from *HMS Ganges* to ask would we do funerals for them if anybody died, and we did one or two. There, we had to dig the grave, then take all the soil away so nobody could see it, and then we would clean the grass all round ready for them to set out their chairs.

DORIS: They used to sit round the grave and sing hymns.

BOB: Those were military funerals, and afterwards they fired their rifles over the grave. They had their own little cemetery at Shotley.

DORIS: Sometimes we would go to Rushmere and dig and get it all ready, then back to Aidringham and dig one there, then back to Shotley – all in one day. We were ever so busy one time, with three graves to dig: so what Bob did was to put my Lambretta in the back of the van and we went to Kesgrave to dig, after which he roped the green mats and the shovels on my Lambretta, and he went off to Nedging Tye (*a small village on the way to Lavenham*) and I went to Felixstowe: so I did mine, and I was back first because Bob's was hard – he had given me the sandy one.

BOB: We had to fill them in: we had dug them both previously. Then we came back to Kesgrave, filled that one in, and that was our day finished.

DORIS: At Whitton (*on the outskirts of Ipswich*) we had to dig one every week: I remember Bob digging a grave and I had to do one on my own: it was a child's grave – we hated doing those.

BOB: You always have so much soil over when you dig a grave, but after a time the surface sinks, so Doris used to do an aftersales service and level them off. Of course, we allowed a hump for the ground to sink, but some places they like to have the surface left flat. One time at Tattingstone there was a dear old man came across from the old people's home, and his toes were out of his boots, and he had been a gravedigger. Wherever you went there was always some man came along who had been a gravedigger: "I used to do that job, mate", he'd say, "but we used to go a lot deeper than that." They had always gone deeper than I did, but whenever I had to reopen any graves I didn't find any deeper than mine. Anyway, this old chap came along when we were just filling in, and I had told Doris to take about six barrowloads away . . .

DORIS: I used to sprinkle it under the hedge.

BOB: We did this to help ourselves, because we always had to rush off somewhere, but this old boy saw me filling in and he said, "You won't get all that back, you know." – "I won't?" – "No, you won't!" – "I bet you half-a-crown I will." – "O.K.", said he, "Half-a-crown – Done!" So we kept filling in, and when we had nearly got all the earth back, the old boy said, "Well, think I'll go and get my tea now", and off he went . . . At times Doris used to get terrible headstrong. One time down at Shotley I said to her, "Don't take the soil away today, please, dear. Don't take any away, because it's very light sandy soil and that'll blow away." – "Oh no, we'll never get all that back. Look at that big heap – we won't get all that back." So she took about six barrowloads and spread it like dust all over the churchyard, and when we were filling in we'd got about two foot more to go and we hadn't got any soil. It took us another couple of hours going all over the churchyard collecting up stones and bits of soil to finish the grave off.

DORIS: One time I was drawing my barrow backwards – they used to get ever so heavy with the clay and stuff – and I went backwards over one of those heaped graves, and the barrow came with me. Sometimes the grave would be

Gravediggers' tea break, Rushmere churchyard 1967

half-full of water, so before the mourners came I would go to a farmyard and gather some bundles of straw or pick piles of grass to go in the bottom.

ERIC: You were going to tell me about the wasp's nest . . .

DORIS: Oh yes, Bob nearly died then. That's the nearest he has ever been to death.

BOB: If I got stung by just one wasp, I swelled up terrible. I never realised then I could get something to counteract the sting.

ERIC: You are allergic?

BOB: That's right. We were over at Polstead, Maria Marten's church, one morning reopening a grave. It was a lovely hot day, so I took my shirt off. I was wearing just trousers and boots, and as I dug I saw what looked like a piece of material in the side of the grave. I poked it with my fork – being summer, the soil was quite hard – and all these wasps came flying out. I dropped everything and ran through the gravestones to where our van was parked, with all these wasps after me, and they stung me all round my stomach and up my chest. Doris was absolutely marvellous. "Please don't panic", she said. "I'll make a cup of tea. Just you sit down quietly", and she went into our van and lit the stove and began making the tea when suddenly I could feel my whole throat swelling up . . .

DORIS: He went absolutely blue. His throat was three times normal size.

BOB: I was choking, and I collapsed – and Doris ran (she told me afterwards) across a field to a house . . .

DORIS: Across *two* fields. I ran, knowing he was unconscious, and I knocked, and this poor woman came to the door, and I said, "For God's sake, get me help – my husband's dying. I think he'll be dead by now!", and I rushed in and there was a Frenchwoman having her breakfast, and I said: "Please come and help me!", so she got in her little sports car – but she had a lot of common sense and rang the doctor before she left. We rushed back, and Bob was still unconscious and we tried to lift him, but he was all covered with sweat and we couldn't manage. Then she said, "I'll get my gardener", and luckily that wasn't an old retired man – in that case, Bob would have been dead, there's no doubt about it – but a big chap, an ex-miner, and he threw Bob in the back among the boards and mats and things and drove to Boxted, and when we got there the doctor rushed out and gave Bob an injection so he could breathe a bit . . .

BOB: It was funny. Subconsciously I knew they had put me in the van, but I was fighting for breath – and then I could feel the needle in my arm, and all at once I was able to breathe again.

DORIS: Then they told us to rush to Sudbury Hospital . . .

BOB: I was unconscious again when we got there.

DORIS: The doctor and the nurse put him on a large trolley, then they laid him on a bed – and "Water!" he kept groaning: and that was about ten in the morning and they wouldn't let me leave the bedside because they said he was never going to pull out of it. He was unconscious until three in the afternoon. "Your husband won't pull through", they told me, "but we'll do our best." And then at 3 p.m. he came to, and said he knew he wasn't dead because he'd still got his boots on! (*She roars with laughter.*)

BOB: There I was, on this bed, with my boots on-and when I came to, I felt marvellous – really great!

DORIS: The doctor said he must stay the night, but Bob said he didn't want that, and he told me, "You'll have to drive." I never had driven our van before, and there were a lot of people about – must have been going to the theatre or something, so Bob lay in the back, and how I got home I don't know – but when we arrived I put him to bed and then I cried for two hours – I just could not stop.

BOB: It was Thursday when this happened, and I was back working again on the Monday. But a week later I was sitting outside Old Felixstowe Church waiting for the hearse to draw up and Mr Reed the churchwarden came along for a chat, and I had my arm outside the window of the van and a wasp settled on me. The sweat dripped down my face and I must have gone white, because he asked, "Do you feel all right, Bob" – and I didn't dare talk until the wasp went. Nowadays, though, I have tablets everywhere, just in case – up there on the shelf, at Aldeburgh, everywhere.

9

"From Milk to the Maltings"

ERIC: When was your first meeting with Ben (*Britten*)?

BOB: Oh, we used to talk to him all the time when he was living at Snape Mill and was along the terrace. I was in the Navy, but Doris was there from 1942. First of all, we lived at Deeker Blower's place, *The Warren*. There was a walk from Ben's mill along Snape Terrace and right down to the river.

DORIS: Before Ben came back from America in summer 1942 Beth Welford (*his sister*) was living at the Mill with her two children. Much later, when we went to help at the concert-hall, George Hardy was in charge, and I have always remembered him saying: "You musn't worry Ben and Peter. They have far too much on their minds, so don't stop them or talk to them." So I would be sweeping along by that little flight of steps leading to the loading-bay and they would come by and I would creech against the wall so they wouldn't have to talk to me. For ages I never spoke to them apart from 'good morning'.

BOB: That only lasted two months, until George Hardy left the Maltings.

ERIC: This was *after* the fire? You went there in April 1971?

BOB: Yes. At the time of the fire we were living in the little bungalow I had renovated along Snape Terrace. We had a card-school with some friends and relations of ours from Leiston, and that night we were having a nice evening

60

together, with some cherry-pies and ham and things like that, and one of the ladies looked out of the window and said: "There's a chimney on fire down the road", and I looked and of course it was the Maltings. I wasn't working there then, so I had no connection with it.

DORIS: You were very cut-up about it, though.

BOB: I phoned the fire-brigade right away, but there had been lots of calls. We could see the flames coming out of the 'bluffers', especially the first one, the east one above the stage. We all stood watching from the terrace – there was nothing anybody could do – and before we separated one of the company said, "You beat us tonight, Bob. We would have to flood Leiston High Street to equal that!"

DORIS: What a sight that was! All those flames – just as though the heat lifted the roof, because it seemed to be suspended in the air above the flames, and then it went down again. That was the illusion from where we were. There were crowds watching from the terrace and when they heard the snapping they thought it was whisky-bottles exploding, not realising it was the asbestos slates on the roof going *bang, bang, bang*!

BOB: It began about 9.30, and it was still burning at eleven o'clock or midnight.

ERIC: How was it you both went to work at the Maltings?

DORIS: We did a milk-round, and we weren't very happy . .

BOB: That was when we left gravedigging. The milkman told us one day there was a job going at Hill Farm Dairy and we thought, "What a nice job! Just putting bottles on doorsteps" – but that turned out the worst job I have ever done in my life. I would rather have carried twelve, sixteen stone of barley from six in the morning until midnight. It was terrible!

DORIS: The repetition . . . !

BOB: Your hands and your clothes were filthy and the old type of van stank of sour milk – God alive! – and a little dog in one place used to bite my leg all the way up the path and all the way back and then the lady would pick it up – (*falsetto*) "Oooh, you little dear! He *loves* you, Bob!" When we left that job, we doubled the milkman's Christmas box. Ugh! What a job! I think you've got to be born to it.

DORIS: There were council-houses in one area with low hedges, and one man wouldn't let us go over them – we walked up his first path, down this one, up another, then back – so early one Sunday morning Bob said: "I'll go!", and he took the milk and jumped the hedges and went right into a pile of empty milk-bottles, and the light went on and a woman called, "Who's that? Who's there?", and we never left any milk because we didn't want her to know who it was.

BOB. We were always getting mixed up, too. Ooh, the people . . . ! "We want two pints on Thursday, and three pints and a pot of cream Friday, and none Saturday" – then next week it's the other way round.

DORIS: We had to go after the bad payers, too. It was hard work.

BOB: One day we were halfway up Kelsale Hill and Doris said something to me and I flew in a rage and jumped in the van and started up – I slammed the clutch in, and it jolted a bit; and there was a crate of gold-tops shot out of the back and they all ran down Kelsale Hill – and Doris said: "You'll have to pay for them!" I had to fork out the cash – and the old boss said, "You're doing well, you two! You've sold a lot of gold-tops."

DORIS: We did more arguing on that job than in our whole lives.

BOB: You left me no end of times. You kept leaving me. "Well, I'm finished", she would say, "I'm not doing any more!" – then she would sulk and stand in the hedge and I'd have to go back and pick her up . . .

DORIS: At Kelsale that morning I had said, "If that's how you feel, I'll get home under my own steam . . .", and Bob said, "You do that, then!", and he pushed the van into gear and I saw the back doors open and the crate half-come out, and then it went back. "Thank goodness!", I thought – then out it came, *CRASH!* This was the early hours of Sunday morning, and the strange thing was there was nobody about and you couldn't see anybody, so we whipped up all the glass and shoved it out of sight – yet during the week they kept on saying, "Last Sunday morning this was a land of milk and honey!" – and everybody knew about it.

BOB: A milkman has to do everything! One old lady before us used to want her mattress turned every so often – they'll stop and do things like that! "Will you do like the other man did – call at the shop and pick me up half a pound of marge and a pound of tea, and bring my newspaper?" Very often, after all, they live in the wilds of the country. One old lady gets the milkman here to do up her corsets or fasten her zip or something! All part of the service – "A pot of cream and two pints of milk and my corsets done up"!

Then the brakes on the van keep going wrong, because you use them constantly. I remember in the middle of Leiston I looked in my offside mirror, then I drew away from the kerb and a car came along – Boum! – and hit me. It was going so fast we were turned right over, and there were we all among the milk-bottles on the ground. It smashed up the van, but we were all right.

They weren't really sorry to see us go – but how it happened we went from milk to the Maltings was, one day we were going to a funeral out Bury St Edmund's way, and my brother-in-law, Iris's husband, asked, "How's the old milk-round going, then?" – "Not very well", I told him. "I don't go a lot on that. I'm getting out as quickly as possible." He told me there was a job going at the Maltings, and next day we went down to see George Hardy, who worked for the Festival. We thought he was the managing director, with his feet up on the desk. They wanted a couple, and "You two will do me fine," he said. He rang Keith Cable (*Secretary of the Aldeburgh Festival*) and Keith cancelled the adverts for the job. So that was the end of the milk-round.

DORIS: We had been going to try window-cleaning next.

BOB: We went over to Aldeburgh for a chat with Stephen Reiss (*General Manager*) and he decided to take us on. But within three months, Stephen was over at Snape, taking off his glasses and wiping them, and saying, "I had a terrible job. I had to sack George." – "Good God!", I said. – Then, "Will you take it on, Bob?", he asked. So there we were, thrown straight into a theatre not so long after a massive fire.

DORIS: What worried me was, we didn't know a thing about it . . . Somebody told us about a door that should either never be shut or never left open, one or the other, and Bob said, "It's like this. I've got to do my job: I *must* find out." And I walked the floor all that night; I would say, "Go in the hall, Bob, and see that's all right" – so of course to keep me quiet he went to the hall a dozen times and came back saying, "Well, that *looks* all right to me . . ."

When he was first told about the job, I said: "It's like this, Bob – I don't want to jump into it like we did the milk round. I don't mind what it is – I love working with you – but I don't want any responsibility", because I don't like responsibility. But the next thing, there we were, and I used to be so worried because we used to have the fire-chiefs down a lot, and even now, although I laugh and carry on, I'll get Bob to go back with me at night, because if that building burned down . . . It isn't an expensive building and you'd get lots of insurance – but everybody loves it, we love it, it's a home for opera, and although I don't understand music, over the years the sound sends hairs up my arms.

BOB: So many people get enjoyment out of it.

DORIS: When the opera is over and the orchestra has gone and you have said, "Goodnight! God bless you! Safe journey home!", there is this lovely building and its foyer so peaceful and quiet, and sometimes that terrifies me . . . I think, if I could only retire now and go up the road and know I've left it safe.

BOB: When we first came here, we had sold the bungalow on the terrace and moved into a house in Aldeburgh, but Ben was anxious for us to move into this flat, which nobody had occupied before. That November we had a big Decca recording in the hall of *The Dream of Gerontius*, and they said, "We'll move the furniture for you". So they brought their big Decca van and moved all our stuff from Aldeburgh.

DORIS: After gravedigging, you can't wonder I found it difficult to relate to the theatre. That was like a gypsy life – absolute freedom. You'd say, "Shall we work late tonight and have a lie-in tomorrow? Or go home now, and get up early?" You were your own boss. – We moved into our Aldeburgh home in June and got new carpets and curtains, and because of the Festival I never had time to look at them. That summer I never got home before two in the morning and we were up again at a quarter to six. So when Bob asked, would I move into the flat at the Maltings, I said: "No, I'm not leaving my own home", but he told me Ben would like us to – so I said: "I'll try it for three months" – and that was fifteen years ago! Sometime later we went past the Aldeburgh house and I said, "Bob, look what the American tenants have done to my new curtains. They've faded them all!" – and he said, "You fool! those are ten years old!" When we left, they were brand new.

ERIC: But you liked the flat?

DORIS: Yes, because in those early days when Bob was working with the English Opera Group, I sometimes had to sleep in the car from 11 p.m to 2 a.m., in the back seat under a coat, and I would wake up shivering. I did that many, many times when they were rehearsing the operas. Sometimes we were up four nights running.

BOB: We used to get lots of opera in those days. One year we had it for a whole month on end.

DORIS: I remember one night – we were in the flat by then – they didn't finish until one in the morning . . .

BOB: During the Colin Graham era *(opera director, who worked closely with Britten's English Opera Group)* . . .

DORIS: "What do you think *you* are doing?", Bob asked me. – "I'm just going to clean the dressing rooms. If I get those done before I go to bed, I shall feel better." – "Leave them!", he told me, getting a bit stroppy. – "No, let me do them, Bob, because they are sure to be here early in the morning." – "*Leave* them!" he said, "Do them tomorrow first thing."

I went to bed and I lay there and I thought about those dressing-rooms and the toilets, and that kept going through my head – so up I got, leaving Bob asleep, and went into the hall and cleaned the whole place from top to bottom – I even swept the foyer on my own. About seven in the morning, I was squeegeeing the last bit of kitchen-floor when out came Bob, yawning. "I overslept", he said, because he was always up by quarter to six. "Oh! *you* overslept! You knew very well I was doing all the work!" So we had a cut-in, Bob is a bit quick-tempered at times. "I don't know what's the matter with you. There's no pleasing you!", he said, and kicked this bucket of dirty water, which went all under the matting – it went everywhere – and he had got this nice white shirt on, while I had been working and was tired – but I squeegeed it up and moved the fridge back all by myself, and I polished the kitchen and the tables and chairs until they looked lovely, then I got my bucket and went upstairs into the restaurant again and Bob was there. "Aaah!", he said, "You've come round, have you? – "You'll come round!", I told him, and I threw the dirty water right over him, and that went all over the tables and chairs. He *looked* . . . ! – then we had another argument – and then he said, "Aren't we a couple of old fools, arguing like this!", and that took us two hours to get it to rights again, for we had to wash all the chairs

Director of scene shifters, c.1975

and put them outside to dry, and wash the tables and the floor – but we were roaring with laughter because it was most unlike me to do a thing like that, because I *never* rebel as a rule.

When we first came to the Maltings – it was after the gravedigging and you can't get anything more basic than that – for the whole first year I knew I was working hard and I knew my legs ached, but there was this feeling I stood on candyfloss, what with the parties and the brightness and the English Opera and all that was going on, and I couldn't help wondering – why am I tired? I was in this party atmosphere, and it took me a year before I really got used to it.

BOB: At Festival times they allocate us some of the Hesse students, a dozen or a half-dozen, but they don't want to do the menial tasks. Nobody wants to help Doris clean the loos or a dressing room – unless it's a star's dressing-room and then only if he is there. They will help us move trees on to the stage, but anything too mundane . . . ! We had one Hesse student – he's a good boy, and now he is a stage-manager at Glyndebourne, but we would say "Just go round this morning and give the door handles a nice rub with Brasso", then you'd come along and see the Brasso and the rag by the door and he would be sitting at the back listening to the rehearsal.

DORIS: When I was younger and when I went out to work, I never listened to music – I was always a great reader. I loved the Brontes and things like that. When we came to the Maltings, I was honest about reading being my thing, not music, and they told me, "You're doing somebody out of a job who would love to be here for the music" – but if I had loved music, *I* would have wanted to be there in the hall, not cleaning the place up afterwards. But I enjoy the concerts now I've been here so long.

BOB: When Ben had a performance at the hall, he used to pop in to see us on the way from his dressing-room, and he'd say, "Get me a whisky, will you, Bob, so I can have a wet when I come off-stage?", and I would pop up to the bar to get him one. Other times he would say, "Come and listen to the bittern", and we would go outside and hear the old bittern booming.

DORIS: When the Queen Mother came here we were cleaning late one night and the bittern was booming away like a foghorn. BOB: We haven't heard one for years – maybe because of the Americans and their *Rod and Gun Club*.

DORIS: There used to be kingfishers, too. Ben was in the restaurant one day and he called, "Doris, come here." So I went to the window and there were two kingfishers.

BOB: He hated to see kids going among the clumps of reeds. That made Ben really furious. He loved to see them left as they were, with no paths between them.

ERIC: I shall never forget Ben's funeral at Aldeburgh in 1976 and you and Bob standing by the graveside, and how you had brought rushes along to line the sides – that was lovely.

BOB: I did one like that at Newbourne with greenery, and there was General Reed at Aldringham, at River Hundred – when his wife was buried, he said to me, "Bob, she didn't like dirt at all, but she loved flowers, so I'll have two vanloads of flowers." I bought some netting and pegged that all round the grave and I threaded all the flowers into the net and barrowed the soil away, and

"Get me a whisky, will you, Bob?" Britten at the Maltings 1971.

there were flowers round the grave, too. For Ben's grave I got hessian and made wire pegs to fasten it against the sides, so that the plumes of the reeds stood up – the top ones were just above the top of the grave. We didn't dig Ben's grave – that was done by the Council – but luckily we knew the lad who was digging it, so I asked him to make it six inches wider all round to allow space for the reeds. Ben always told us he wanted to be buried at the Maltings. One day we were in the flat and Bill Servaes (*General Manager of the Aldeburgh Festival*) was there, and Lilias and Robin Sheepshanks had brought the Colonel down from the American Air Force base at Bentwaters, and Ben said, "I want Bob and Doris to bury me, and I want to be buried in the reeds over here." But this isn't consecrated ground, of course, and his family and everyone wanted him to be buried at Aldeburgh, so Bill Servaes thought the next best thing would be to lay some reeds in the grave. Then one night Doris and I were lying in bed talking and we though of the idea of lining the whole grave with reeds.

ERIC: You were going to tell me about going up the Street after the keys.

DORIS: That happened not very long ago.

BOB: When Sir Eugene Melville became Chairman of the Aldeburgh Foundation, we were invited to Aldeburgh one night for drinks. We were going on holiday next morning, so I wanted to make a good start and leave about 4 a.m. My brother-in-law Neville was going to be our relief, and I had left my set of keys for him with some friends in the village, and Doris had *her* set.

We got home about ten, and there was a tent and a car outside on the grass, so I said to Doris, "We can't have him camping there." We don't allow anyone to camp, and if the police had come along they would probably have knocked me up to ask why he was there. I went over and told the man he would have to move to a camping-site down the road. He grumbled a bit, but finally he agreed. He started up his car and drove it to the top of the wall and I left him packing his gear with the headlights full on.

We'd more or less got into bed, when we heard *bang bang* on the door, and there was this massive chap – I hadn't been able to see him until then – and his wife or girlfriend was with him, and he said, "Can you give us a push? The car won't start. I've run the battery down." I just pulled on a pair of trousers, with nothing on my top, and went outside. Doris didn't know what was happening, so she followed me out in her shortie nightie, when suddenly *Bang!* the door shut. So there we were on the doorstep with a locked door behind us. I gave the chap a push to get the engine running, then I asked, "Will you give us a lift up to the Street?", and he looked a bit cross about it after being turned off the place, but we both piled into the back of his little VW as far as the *Crown*, and from there we walked up the hill to our friend who had the keys. It was past midnight by this time, so they were in bed – and there were the two of us shivering away, Doris in her nightie, me with my bare top, and both of us without shoes. Charlie and Rosemary came to the door and I got the keys, then he said, "Well, you can walk back now." – "*NO!*", I said, and finally he agreed to bring us home. Afterwards, of course, we had a real good laugh about it.

10

"I'll walk round with Bob"

BOB: When the Queen Mum came down to open the Britten-Pears School *(in 1979)*, the first question she asked of Peter *(Pears)* was, "How did they build those lovely brick ceilings?" He said, "Well Bob knows all about it." So she said, "Well I'll walk round with Bob and you follow us."

That instant rapport was typical of the way that Bob and Doris endeared themselves to everyone, including Britten and Pears themselves and the many famous musicians who worked and performed at Snape. Doris corresponded with Britten while he was in hospital for a heart operation in 1973, and there is an evocative photo of Bob and Ben and his nurse, Rita Thomson, taken the following year. It's an image of friendship. Other photos, of Bob with the cellist 'Slava' Rostropovich and with Hugh Maguire (Director of Strings at the Britten-Pears School) testify to the sense of fun that seemed to surround them, the camaraderie.

The news of their retirement, in 1989, was greeted with loving dismay. Princess Margaret of Hesse & the Rhine (President of the Aldeburgh Foundation) sent a telegram that summed up the feelings of everyone who worked with them. "Dear Bob – you and Doris belong to all of us, Aldeburgh and Snape for ever and ever. We can't do without you."

The Queen Mother visits the Maltings, 1979

Friends – Bob with Ben Britten and his nurse, Rita Thomson

Pals – Bob with the great cellist, 'Slava' Rostropovich

Jokers – Bob with Hugh Maguire, Director of Strings at the Britten Pears School

11

An evening at The Crown

These reminiscences by Bob and Doris were recorded during the winter of 1985/86. I sent a copy of the transcript to a friend, Simon Loftus. He replied with this letter.

Eric Crozier

I am writing this now as quickly as I can so as not to forget it. We have just come back from dinner at The Crown with Hugh Maguire and Tricia, and Bob and Doris. It was of course the most enjoyable and hilarious evening, and I *wish* I had been able to tape Doris in full flow because I have never heard her talk so wonderfully and the whole tenor of their conversation was like the most tremendous love story, with that extraordinary mixture of really earthy tenderness which I have never heard so directly and unconsciously expressed by anyone else. Two moments in particular stuck in my mind and I wanted to tell you about them because I am not sure that they have yet surfaced in the tapes which you have recorded.

One was another gravedigging story. Bob was talking about the problem of digging a double grave in dry, hot weather. The gravediggers often did not dig down the full six foot six inches for the first coffin, so when some years later you reopened the grave to put the second coffin in there wasn't sufficient depth. Once, when he and Doris were digging out such a grave they encountered the problem – they only got down about three foot when they hit the first coffin.

So they dug that out too, bits and pieces of bones and wood, and hid the bits behind a bush during the funeral service. Afterwards, when everyone had gone home, they tossed the bits and pieces back on top of the second coffin and filled in the grave. "So instead of David lying on top of Mabel, it was Mabel lying on top of David!"

The other glorious moment was after Hugh had asked how they met and Doris had told the courtship story. She then went on about how her mother was so strict – her family was Methodist, but Bob's were church – and about how "when we were young none of us girls were ever allowed to see our brothers in their vests even, and they never saw their sisters in their petticoats. I had no idea what a man looked like, that's the truth. So when I saw Bob he was the first man I ever did see naked, and it's wonderful isn't it? Well it is. I still think the sight of a man naked is so lovely." (All this, of course, without anything but a sort of passionate, dreamy directness – no innuendos.) "So Bob was the first man I ever saw, and when I touched him I was overwhelmed. I suppose we've got something to thank Mum for, after all, because if she hadn't been so strict I might not have been so struck by Bob – I'd have thought he was normal. He was only fifteen, but what a man he was! I was *determined* to have him."

The way both of them talk is, of course, amazing – especially Doris – but the way they listen to what the other is saying about them – especially Bob – is what I find increasingly moving. In a way that's hard to convey to those who don't know them, theirs is one of the great love stories.

S. L.

12

Postscript: Letters from Doris

Doris wrote the most wonderful letters – pungent, immediate, with a relish for life and instinctive wisdom. Everyone who received them kept them, including Benjamin Britten and his long-standing associate (and joint Artistic Director of the Aldeburgh Festival) Imogen Holst – as I discovered on a recent visit to the Britten-Pears Archive. I decided to include a few extracts in this new edition.

S. L.

To Benjamin Britten

The first few letters were written when Britten was in hospital in London for his heart operation – and the last was sent a few months before his death.

8 April 1973

Dear Ben,

It's very quiet here this morning after the activity of last evening's concert, the clouds are low and moving slowly past the window and yet there is a great deal of movement with the birds swooping low and the reeds all of a tizzy in the wind – my word it's now started to hail and a couple of men on the wall are hurrying over the stile, I bet it's stinging to their faces. Isn't it good to feel in this changing world the view from here is almost exactly as it was so many years ago.

I had a very restless night. I got up at four to make a pot of tea and how reassuring it was to stand on the step and see the large outline of the hall black in the morning light as it should be and I realised how much you must often be awake with works you are composing and was glad you had the opera *(Death in Venice)* finished, for isn't it a nuisance when your brain won't let the other parts of you relax and sleep.

The hail has now stopped beating on the windows and the courtyard to the flat is covered with overgrown hundreds and thousands like the coloured ones we used to buy when we were children at Mrs Baggot's shop.

We are looking forward to your return to the Maltings again soon, all ready to enjoy your music.

Love Doris & Bob

Britten replied on 15 April

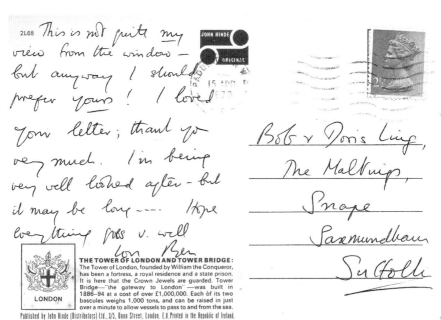

This is not quite my view from the window — but anyway I should prefer yours! I loved your letter; thank you very much. I'm being very well looked after – but it may be long –––– Hope everything goes v. well

Love Ben

Bob & Doris Ling,
The Maltings,
Snape,
Saxmundham,
Suffolk

THE TOWER OF LONDON AND TOWER BRIDGE: The Tower of London, founded by William the Conqueror, has been a fortress, a royal residence and a state prison. It is here that the Crown Jewels are guarded. Tower Bridge—"the gateway to London"—was built in 1886–94 at a cost of over £1,000,000. Each of its two bascules weighs 1,000 tons, and can be raised in just over a minute to allow vessels to pass to and from the sea.

Published by John Hinde (Distributors) Ltd., 3/5, Dunn Street, London. E.8. Printed in the Republic of Ireland.

8 May 1973

Dear Ben,

After Easter we had such glorious days weatherwise, the sun shone and the outside of the hall looked lovely, the grass cut and the daffodils out and the gorse bright on the distant heathland it must have given great pleasure to the many people strolling around. Last Friday we had such a severe storm, I expect you heard it too, as it was coming up it looked as if it was skimming the marshes, maybe because the clouds were so low. I was jolly thankful when the tide drew that away, storms being my least favourite of the elements. We hear the cuckoo and the Bittern regularly now and no end of duck gather on the water.

Bob and I have had a few days off and we have been using the time to clear out Bob's shed that has held things that might come in handy, for over thirty years. We've made several trips to the council tip at Yoxford and watched a lifetime's collection engulfed in a mechanical monster that seemed to swallow everything from bed springs, old boots and settees, and its regular rhythm gives no indication of any digestive troubles.

December 1973

Dear Ben,

Thank you for your kindness letting us know you would be unable to attend our party, we would have loved you to have been there yet knew it would have been most unwise, but I knew inside myself that your best wishes were with us and that was more than enough for us.

We did enjoy our party, the preparing for it as well as actually the party itself, it's always the same with me I plan to be elegant and look after my guests, but in no time at all I'm having such a good time myself, the time slips away and after its over I think 'oh my goodness I've done it again'.

On the Sunday lunch time we had another lovely time, for our old Decca lads *(the team from Decca records)* hadn't had any of my plum pudding so they came up, and we had a meal of the leftovers and I heated up another pudding and we had a hilarious time, we missed them when they went.

2 Jan 1975

Dear Ben,

I do hope you enjoyed your Christmas, looking back over the years I think this was our very best ever. The weather was so perfect, we walked the river walls and marshes and the clouds and sun would need to be seen to be appreciated. Wasn't the moonlight wonderful on new year's Eve, we had a party before our clan went back to their own homes, we drew up the blinds, the coloured lights shone on the window and the moonlight came flooding through the top windows, how our Auld Lang Syne sounded to the wild life outside I don't know, but I felt so grateful that we had been blessed with such a happy time, so now we're all ready and waiting and hoping for a happy season in the hall. Please wish Peter and everyone a happy new year from us both.

June 1976

Dear Ben,

In case I should miss seeing you, Bob and I were so happy to read of your award this morning, not just for all you've achieved but also because it's you. *(Britten was awarded a life peerage a few months before his death).*

To Imogen Holst

'Imo' became friends with Doris, after Britten's death, and would give her a book token at Christmas. These two letters were written in thanks.

December 1982 (?)

Dear dear Imogen,

Bob has enjoyed the last few days getting the Christmas trees from Tangham Forest and arranging them on stage. I had to laugh for Chris *(Nicholson)*, Harry *(Pipe)* and Bob had an early coffee then set off with spades and sacks in case they got stuck, just like young schoolboys all excited. Ages after they came back like they were ninety, having had to pull and heave the trees due to not being able to get the van up the track, but they thought it still a huge joke. As they were late the chaps stayed at the flat for fish and chips, and I'm always being asked for a plum duff so I took them at their word and that's what they had for pudding with custard, it was quite a hilarious lunch time. The trees do look nice, the one on the outside is lit up and looks lovely from the village and the three on stage look pretty too. Bob is in his glory doing things like that.

Happy at work. Bob & Doris with Chris Nicholson and Harry Pipe, 1984.

Do you remember my telling you of my granddaughter and her little friend doing a Ballet show here in the flat? It was as moving an experience as anyone could wish for. They spent all afternoon arranging the seats, making out the two tickets and programmes for Bob and me, and I dressed up in a long dress and shawl. I don't suppose the dancing was up to a very high standard, but the expressions on their faces of love, pity, disdain and anger had to be seen to be believed. They put their all into it. . . With the music of the ballet on the radiogram, low lights and those children I felt quite cold with emotion.

December 1983

Dear Imogen

As I expect you know reading is one of the best things in my life. I often thank God for books for when life has been difficult and thoughts hard to bear as we all get in this life (for we wouldn't enjoy or appreciate the white bits if there weren't black would we) then I've been able to lose myself in a book for a blessed respite and found things a lot easier afterwards, as I know you do with music. I often ponder over music for with reading you know and can understand what you read, but with music I know what moves me, makes me go cold or excited and even if low could drive me almost to suicide but I don't know why or what it does, it's all a great mystery to me.

Yesterday we came to Aldeburgh and walked to the Martello Tower and I felt near to my dad for he used to be there in the great war, and my dear mum bringing up us thirteen children and granny all in a little tiny two bedroomed cottage and an attic. How easily mother could have been feckless with all of us but the memories of our warm home, marvellous food, and the cleanliness of it all, she deserved a medal as big as a frying pan. There was always room at the table for our friends and I don't ever remember hearing her grumble, what grand parents we had.

Yesterday afternoon the view from the windows here was breath taking, after the morning rain the sun came out and over the marshes everything had a yellow golden hue, right now it's grey and with a Margaret Catchpole feeling, like the human face there's something different every time.